The 40 Best Sales Techniques Ever

CONQUER THE LEADERBOARD, CRASH PRESIDENT'S CLUB, AND MAKE MORE MONEY

JONATHAN JEWETT (MY NEPHEW)!

Editor: Patricia Bull

Cover design: D.V. Suresh

Publishing Brand Consultant: Helen Chang

CAMLAN PRESS

D0840992

This book is dedicated to my father, John P. Jewett—

Dad, I wrote this book for both of us.

MY

BROTHER-in-LAW

"The credit belongs to the man who is actually in the arena, whose face is marred by dust and sweat and blood; who strives valiantly; who errs, who comes short again and again, because there is no effort without error and shortcoming; who spends himself in a worthy cause; who at the best knows in the end the triumph of high achievement, and who at the worst, if he fails, at least fails while daring greatly, so that his place shall never be with those cold and timid souls who neither know victory nor defeat."

- Theodore Roosevelt Jr., 26th U.S. President

"Rules are in every company for everyone to follow.
Eh, except salespeople."

- Jeffrey Gitomer, Author and Sales Guru

Author Dedication to his uncle

Thanks for reading.

Contents

INTRODUCTION

Sales is a Hard Job

As I step into the CEO's office for our weekly meeting, I immediately notice the CFO seated at the conference table. This is unexpected. Both he and the CEO wear what can only be described as very solemn expressions.

Uh-oh, I thought. *This can't be good.*

The CEO-Founder had hired me six months earlier to run the sales department of his small software company. I use the term "sales department" loosely because it was really just myself and another individual who'd been tending to sales prior to my arrival and was prone to regular emotional meltdowns. Rather than discussing his [lack of] deals, I often found myself talking him down from the ledge and wishing I could just fire him.

But of course I knew why the CFO was there.

I agreed to take this role because at first it appeared to be a terrific opportunity to build and run a young sales organization and advance my career. What I quickly discovered was that not all software was the same, and the product—a niche business-intelligence platform for real estate companies—demanded a working knowledge of a market that I knew nothing about. Every aspect of the value proposition, customers and market were utterly foreign to me. I would regularly drag the CEO out on sales calls to compensate for my shortcomings, but after six months I had not made a single sale. It was painfully obvious that the current situation was untenable. The "sales" department wasn't selling.

The CEO got right down to it. "You've been here six months," he said, peering at me over his glasses. "And we don't have any revenue to show for it."

Yeah, I thought. *Your product's way too expensive. The market sucks. Nobody supports me. Leads are non-existent. The sales cycle's too long. My "team" is a joke.* Every excuse that I had made to him—and myself—for the past six months floated through my mind.

The CEO continued. "What the hell is going on? You need to make a sale, fast, or I'm letting you go."

THUD. There it was.

I was put on a 45-day performance plan with a $300,000 target. I thought I stood a better chance of scaling Mount Everest in rollerblades. I had been on sales performance plans before, and put many of my own direct reports on performance plans, and it's never a comfortable place to be. There are two possible outcomes:

Outcome #1 is that that you dig down, find the mental toughness to meet the challenge head-on and work tirelessly to make your number. I've seen performance plans awaken the sleeping giant in some people, who then went on to become my best reps.

Outcome #2 is that you mentally check out from the job and start calling around for your next job.

My choice was #1. My wife tells me that I'm a Type A personality disguised as Type B, and I would have to agree with her. I'd rather catch flies with honey than vinegar, but you can damn well bet that I'm catching those flies. Even though I knew deep down that this company wasn't for me, just throwing in the towel seemed out of the question.

As soon as the meeting was over, I pulled out a legal pad and started brainstorming every idea I could possibly think of to magically produce $300K in 45 days. I initially came up with about 20 ideas, and, over time, I added 20 additional ideas. Together, they would become the best practices presented in *The 40 Best Sales Techniques Ever*.

These techniques are the sharpest tools in my sales toolbox, and have been refined during my 22-year career selling enterprise software to Fortune 500 companies. My background is B2B sales, and I've always sold my products to corporate customers. That said, I've done my best to broaden the appeal of *The 40 Best* and make them relevant for reps selling in B2C and other environments. These techniques are based on universal selling principles, and I'm confident they'll work whether your buyer is a corporation, partner, association, or individual.

I can personally vouch for the effectiveness of *The 40 Best*. I've used all of them to find new business, accelerate sales cycles, and get customers to sign on the dotted line. Each technique is designed to bring creativity, daring, innovation, and velocity to your deals. When applied skillfully, *The 40 Best* will become your ticket to greater job satisfaction, bigger commission checks and the professional success we're all striving to achieve.

I've always been a professional salesman. I've always operated under the tremendous pressure that comes with carrying a sales quota. With the exception of a brief stint selling radio advertising—where I made my sales bones because you either sold or you starved—I've spent my entire career in software sales. In good years, I was a top producer who exceeded my quota and saw my name in lights atop the leaderboard. I took all-expense-paid trips to Hawaii and Puerto Rico as part of President's Club.[1] I cashed big commission checks, and there were years when I made more money than anyone else in my company—including the CEO.

But I've also lost my share of deals; failed more times than I can remember; been fired for missing my quota; gotten chewed out for sub-par results; had prospects call my boss demanding that I be replaced; and taken the dreaded "perp walk" through the office with my box of belongings, staring shamefully at the floor while my [former] colleagues whispered behind my back.

Believe me, President's Club is better.

---

[1] President's Club goes by many names, and is the recognition of a company's top sales performers. Achievers are often awarded trips, cash, cars, stock and other perks.

So how does one succeed in sales? First, you need to be able to convince other people to give you their money. The more, the better. Second, you need to perform. Third, you need an arsenal of sales weapons at your disposal that can be brought to bear when you need them. **Serendipity and the kindness of strangers won't help you to conquer the leaderboard and crash President's Club, but *The 40 Best* will**. My hope is that this book is the first step in your transformation from promising rep into unstoppable sales juggernaut.

Let's face it, sales is a hard job. I contend that it's the most difficult job in any company. Ninety-nine percent of people couldn't do what we do. Intel's Andy Grove once remarked that "only the paranoid survive," and it's certainly true in our profession. All of us are only as good as our last deal. We may kill our number this year, only to see the big board reset back to zero on January 1st. There's a reason that the sales group experiences higher turnover than any other department—many people just can't hack it. To be in sales is to accept a constant level of paranoia and operate on the razor's edge between hero and zero *every single day.*

On the other hand, sales is the fuel that keeps the engines of commerce running. Our tribe is large and fierce. We deal with negativity and rejection that would cause lesser people to crumble. We keep a stiff upper lip with unreasonable customers whom we'd rather just push off a balcony. We run complex and difficult sales cycles that require us to juggle dozens of moving parts, all of which can come crashing down at any moment. When we win, we get credit. When we lose, we get the blame. We like the money— who wouldn't—but we sure as hell earn it.

Now think about this for a moment…

Although the sales function is vital to every company's survival, our system of higher education pays virtually no attention to preparing students for a sales career. Harvard Business School Professor Walter Friedman wrote a book called *Birth of a Salesman,* in which he states:

While business schools have continued to offer some type of sales management instruction—usually within a larger marketing course—**they do not offer courses in salesmanship skills**. The topic remains, just as it was in the 1910s, more suitable for popular how-to books and memoirs of successful salespeople than for academic classes.

Unlike our colleagues in Finance, Marketing, HR, Operations and IT, we sales professionals cannot rely on universities to teach us the basic tenets of our craft. Sales classes are virtually non-existent, and there is no degree in sales. Instead, ours is the School of Hard Knocks; we're forced to be self-reliant and learn through hand-to-hand combat on the front lines of business. This lack of institutional support, in my opinion, is a major reason why parents don't encourage their kids to enter the sales profession. How many girls and boys aspire to be salespeople when they grow up? Not many, and I'd speculate that most people either wander or fall into sales as a career. It's a shame, because you can build a very good life for yourself in this business and have some fun along the way.

There's much speculation about the "digital economy" and what it means to the modern worker. It's been estimated that up to 47% of all employment in the United States could be vulnerable to automation in the next 20 years. One model predicts that good jobs will be replaced by two kinds of jobs: minimum-wage jobs and "sharing economy" jobs, represented by companies like Uber and Airbnb. Although the outlook is depressing for most workers, it's difficult to see the demand for skilled salespeople ever subsiding. Companies will always need ambassadors at the front lines of business, overcoming objections and getting buyers to open their wallets. **As a sales professional, you should take comfort in the fact that your future is *more* secure than that of many of your peers. As long as you can sell, that is.**

So, why should you read this book, and what's in it for you?

If you want to make more money, this book is for you.

If you're managing a sales team, this book is for you.

If you're an executive responsible for results and you believe your sales team can do even better, this book is for you.

If you're on a performance plan, this book is for you.

If you want to smash through the constraints that have stopped you from reaching your full potential, this book is for you.

If you want to test yourself, improve your craft and add even sharper arrows to your sales quiver, this book is for you.

The salespeople I've taught to use *The 40 Best* have been trained in a variety of sales methodologies: SPIN Selling; Solution Selling; Consultative Selling; the Challenger Sale; Strategic Selling; or a hybrid of these models. **The good news is that *The 40 Best* work no matter what sales philosophy you follow**. These are tactics to help you handle the situations you encounter every day with greater skill, and their appeal is universal. My intent was not to create yet another trendy sales system, but to **detail specific actions that you can take *immediately* to improve your sales performance.**

The inimitable Dale Carnegie wrote the following in the introduction to his classic 1936 book, *How to Win Friends and Influence People*:

> If by the time you have finished reading the first three chapters of this book—if you aren't then a little better equipped to meet life's situations, then I shall consider this book to be a total failure so far as you are concerned. For the great aim of education is not knowledge but action. And this is an action book.

***The 40 Best Sales Techniques Ever* is an action book.** You're reading it because you want better results, so what can you expect? I won't go so far as to say *The 40 Best* will defy the laws of sales physics, but I will state that these techniques can improve every aspect of your sales performance. They're designed specifically to empower salespeople to find, drive, and close business as quickly as possible. I can't guarantee results, of course, but I can guarantee that doing the same thing will generate the same outcome. Likewise, I can guarantee you that doing nothing will produce nothing.

We all want to supercharge our careers, and this is certainly why I read sales books. I have one major complaint about the genre, however: most of them present various sales frameworks and models, yet contain very little information on how to translate sales theory into actual results. Books about sales theory outnumber those about execution by a significant margin. Most authors are so busy proselytizing at 10,000 feet that they miss the action on the ground, and this is truly where Sales lives and breathes.

The authors make a very compelling case, backed up by charts, graphs, statistics, surveys and interviews, but I'm always left with the same thought: *sounds good on paper, but how can it help me make more money?* Monday morning arrives, and without a concrete plan of action, I fall right back into my old habits. I became so fed up with this pointless cycle that I decided to take a different approach with this book: forget sales theory, and instead provide lots of practical steps, templates, and how-to guides you can use *on your very next sales call.*

I have lived every single one of *The 40 Best*. If there was a technique or approach that helped me to close more deals and make more money, it's included in this book. ***The 40 Best*** have increased my confidence and elevated my sales game. I firmly believe that I could parachute into virtually any company and apply these techniques to increase sales. More important, I can teach other salespeople—like you—to wield these techniques with maximum effectiveness, and it doesn't matter whether you sell software, insurance, consulting or corporate jets.

Of course, you don't have to take my word for it. In fact, I highly recommend that you field-test every one of ***The 40 Best*** yourself. The techniques are specifically designed to be actionable, and there's no reason you couldn't begin experimenting with them on your next customer call. As you become more skilled and comfortable with ***The 40 Best***, I have no doubt that you'll give them your own unique spin and truly make them your own. Over time, these best practices will become like second nature to you, and you'll start seeing the benefits of operating at a higher level in your sales career.

Here's your first assignment: go out and buy a sturdy notebook and write "Sales Journal" on the front (Evernote works too). Your sales journal will become your source for all things sales, and every lesson, reflection, revelation and inspiration should be committed to its pages. Unless you have a voluminous memory, writing things down is the best way to make sure that nothing important gets lost. Make the sales journal a constant companion on your journey and review it regularly to refresh yourself and keep your skills sharp.

Many salespeople have told me that *The 40 Best* really work, and that these techniques have become part of their daily routine. Their value is proven in terms of more deals closed, more commissions paid, sales quotas met, and promotions earned. It should be easy to measure your progress, because you're either closing deals and generating more revenue or you're not. This is really the eternal paradox of sales:

The good news is that you always know where you stand.

The bad news—especially if you're not closing—is that you always know where you stand.

You're probably wondering what happened with the CEO and my performance plan. I ended up closing 55% of the $300K target—about $165K—which was $165K more than I thought I could close. Despite my progress, the CEO and I agreed that this job wasn't a good fit for me and my performance plan became an exit plan.

What this experience taught me was that I could spin my wheels cold-calling, or I could master proven techniques that gave me a much better shot at meeting my goals. I left this job with the beginnings of *The 40 Best* scribbled in my notebook, and a strong feeling that I was really onto something.

I take great pleasure in being a salesman. It's not the easiest or safest job in the world, but none of our colleagues have a more thrilling ride than we do. We're the CEOs of our own business, and our destiny rests in our hands. We get to travel, and we don't have to stare at the same four walls every day. Master the art of selling and you'll make a good living; fail and you'll be searching for a new career. If you want to ride the merry-go-round, go into Marketing. If you're just crazy enough to hang on to the roller coaster, then Sales is for you.

Ours is an honorable profession, so never let anyone tell you otherwise. **Remember, *you* pay everyone's salary**. Reading this book and learning how to use *The 40 Best* is one more step along your path to sales greatness. Have fun and enjoy the ride, because as the eminently quotable Steve Jobs once said, "The journey is the reward."

I'd very much like to hear about your experiences with *The 40 Best*. Visit my website (The40Best.com) and drop me a note to let me know how you're doing. I'll post your stories and comments to the blog and share them on social media.

I wish you well on this journey. Here's to your success!

Jonathan Jewett

How to Use This Book: 8 Tips

1. I'll refer to the forty techniques in this book as *The 40 Best*. The book is not sequential in terms of learning, since each of *The 40 Best* is designed to be a stand-alone technique. In theory, you could start at #38 and jump to #5 or #17. Practically, however, I recommend reading through all forty techniques before deciding which of them you'd like to try first.

2. Read the book from front to back, highlighting the techniques and passages that interest you. This will enable you to later review important sections much more quickly. Once you've finished the book, re-read the highlighted sections thoroughly and choose a manageable number of techniques to get started. Work on these until you've mastered them, and then choose a new series of techniques to execute.

3. With a few exceptions, each technique follows the same format:

    *   **Introduction**: A summary of the technique and the outcome it's designed to achieve.
    *   **Game Prep**: The steps you should take to prepare before you execute on the technique.
    *   **Showtime**: Your plan to put the technique into action.

    Resist the urge to jump right into *Showtime* before you're ready; you'll be much more effective when you take the time to fully understand the technique and complete the prep work.

4. Look for every opportunity to apply *The 40 Best* in your daily routine. As you become more proficient, personalize each technique to fit your own selling style. In this way, you'll truly own these techniques and transform them into best practices that will become, over time, second nature.

5. Make *The 40 Best Sales Techniques Ever* your constant companion and a working reference handbook. Keep this book

handy and commit to review and try new techniques regularly. For example, let's assume you've committed to try four new techniques every month (one per week). On this timeline, you can conquer the leaderboard, earn your place at President's Club, and make more money within a year. Not bad at all.

6. Track your progress. Ultimately, every one of *The 40 Best* is about driving better outcomes and results. In sales, the usual success metrics are more revenue, bigger commissions, more deals closed, shorter sales cycles, and greater customer satisfaction. Think about how you're going to measure your success with each technique, and track your results in your Sales Journal. If you find that a technique is working for you, keep doing it. If it's not working, change your approach or try a new technique.

7. A quick terminology note: I use the terms **customer, prospect,** and **client** to indicate different types of buyers. **Customers** have made a purchase from you and are actively using your products or services. **Prospects** have never bought from you before; many of *The 40 Best* are intended to help you convert prospects into customers. **Client** is used as a generic term, meaning that the technique could apply to both customers and prospects. I point this out because certain techniques are designed to work with certain types of buyers. Selling to customers, who already know and trust you is much different than making a first-time sale to a new prospect. I've done my best to use the right term to indicate the type of buyer each technique should be targeting.

8. Have fun, and don't be dissuaded by the occasional setback (you're trying something new, after all). Work hard and keep your eyes on the prize, and you'll succeed in sales, business, and life in general.

PART ONE

"Think Different"

Many of you may recall Apple's famous "Think Different" ad campaign, in which a picture montage of Albert Einstein, Bob Dylan, Martin Luther King Jr., Thomas Edison and Pablo Picasso float across the screen while a narrator intones, ". . . and while some may see them as the crazy ones, we see genius. Because the people who are crazy enough to think they can change the world, are the ones who do."

Unless you challenge yourself, you'll never know what you're truly capable of achieving. Bucking the status quo requires courage, confidence and a willingness to try and sometimes fail. This can be difficult in a sales organization, where conformity is often prized. It can also be stated, however, that top salespeople don't beat the leaderboard because they studied the sales manual harder than anyone else. Instead, "they are the crazy ones, the misfits, the rebels, the troublemakers. They're not fond of rules, and they have no respect for the status quo."

The techniques in Part One challenge you to "think different"; to step outside your comfort zone, challenge yourself, and open your mind to new ideas about how you can drive sales results. Although it's easy and comfortable to coast along on cruise control, it's much harder (but more exciting) to drive in the fast lane. This is how you stand out and produce outstanding results. **Our goal as salespeople is not to achieve somewhat-competent mediocrity; it's to climb the leaderboard, secure our spot in President's Club, and make more money.**

The 7 techniques presented in **"Think Different"** are:

#1: Rewrite the Rulebook
The salesperson who writes the rules controls the game. You need to write (or rewrite) the rules of every customer engagement.

#2: Shred the Box
Don't just think outside the box—shred it into a million pieces. Approach every day—and every deal—with a spirit of innovation and creativity, and the business will follow.

#3: Three New Ideas
Winners bring big, bold ideas to the table and passionately advocate for them. Once you've closed the blockbuster deals, you'll never settle for small deals again.

#4: Go Looking for Trouble
Companies in trouble need help—fast. Their urgency can become your opportunity if you know where and how to go looking for trouble.

#5: Read the Tea Leaves
Change happens whether you welcome it or dread it. Smart salespeople try to anticipate the future and think about how they can create opportunity in a shifting business landscape.

#6: New Faces
It's frustrating when your deal is stuck. Bringing in the right people at the right time can be exactly what you need to get your deal back on track and win the business.

#7: The Tip of the Iceberg
What if I told you that your approach to handling objections was completely wrong? Objections are only the tip of the iceberg; your true risk factors are lying in wait just beneath the surface, and they'll shipwreck your deal unless you find the underlying risks and eliminate them.

#1: Rewrite the Rulebook

The salesperson who writes the rules controls the game. You need to write (or rewrite) the rules of every customer engagement.

Have you ever received an RFP that reads as if it's been written by one of your competitors? If the answer is Yes, it's because the RFP probably *was* written by one of your competitors. Although buyers have access to more research than ever before, many of them go shopping for new products without fully understanding and defining their own needs first. This is a perfect opportunity for a helpful vendor (like you) to take their hand and guide them to an inevitable conclusion: that *you* are the best partner to work with.

Rewrite the Rulebook details how you can exert significant influence over the buyer and essentially write their requirements in a way that favors you. If a buyer shows up with their requirements and buying process fully defined, you'll have to play by their rules. But, when the buyer needs help (as most of them do) and is amenable to your guidance, you can write the rules of the game in your favor and set yourself up to win. This technique is about controlling the sales cycle, shutting out the competition, and giving yourself an unfair advantage in the sales cycle.

To succeed, you need to reach prospects early in their process (while they can still be influenced) and provide what I call a "starter kit" of information and materials to move them down your preferred path. If the prospect hasn't fully defined their requirements yet, you give them a comprehensive list of requirements as their foundation. If they've never bought a product like yours before, you hand them a guide to evaluating and buying your product. If they're unsure about building the business case to justify the purchase, you point them toward case studies and a Return-on-Investment (ROI) calculator that clearly defines the financial benefits of investing with you.

Very simply, you're setting yourself up to win the game because you're writing the rules. In most cases, people will gladly accept your help because you're reducing their workload and saving them time. You're building trust and showcasing your expertise. You're shutting out the competition because *your* product features have become *the buyer's* product features, leading to the inevitable conclusion that *you* are the right solution to their problems. This technique will fundamentally change your approach to new business development and enable you to take control of the sales cycle beginning with the very first conversation.

* GAME PREP *

Rewrite the Rulebook requires you to be proactive and take control of the sales cycle. This starts with the discovery process. Rather than sleepwalking through discovery, you want to actively shape the prospect's perceptions and requirements. The challenge is that good discovery can be limited by the amount of time a prospect is willing and able to spend with you. **The key to securing quality time with a prospect is to deliver value in every call, email, and meeting.** Teaching the prospect something they don't already know is a great way to get their attention and make sure that you become a priority.

The **Customer Starter Kit** is your secret weapon to deliver value, become a priority, and begin to influence the prospect's thinking. It's a portfolio of relevant documents and resources that both provide value and nudge the prospect in your direction, and it should be introduced on you're the very first call with a new prospect. While your business will develop its own custom Starter Kit, here's a list of five resources to get you started:

1. Requirements List
2. Evaluation Plan
3. Deployment Roadmap
4. ROI Calculator
5. Targeted Case Studies

Requirements List

Often derived from past RFP responses, the Requirements List is a checklist of the features and functions that a typical company buying your solution *should* be looking for. If the prospect has already created this list, ask them to share it with you, as it will reveal exactly how to sell them. If, like most prospects early in the diligence process, they haven't defined their requirements yet, it creates a huge advantage for you. Why? Because the Requirements List is heavily weighted in your favor. *Your* list of features and functions becomes *their* list of features and functions. Even if the prospect modifies this document, their final requirements will likely be very similar to those provided by you.

Commonly, the Requirements List is created as an Excel spreadsheet. The Y-axis lists all the key features and functions that a solution needs to possess, and the X-axis lists my company and two generic competitors in separate columns. The spreadsheet format lends itself perfectly to a side-by-side comparison of all vendors. You might be thinking that I'm breaking sales rule #1 by introducing competitors into my sales cycle. You're right—except I don't fear the competition *because I wrote the requirements.* **Since I define the requirements as everything my product does well, I know that no competitor will ever beat me.** I can afford to present the *impression* of a fair comparison because in reality it's a deck fully stacked in my favor.

Evaluation Plan

The Evaluation Plan provides the prospect with a detailed roadmap to buy your product, laying out the key activities that normally occur when a prospect is evaluating a product like yours. This can be especially helpful if you're selling to a business unit that's new to the process and doesn't often make product purchases. To create this document, write down the usual steps followed by most buyers and supplement this with information specific to your buying cycle.

For example, here's an Evaluation Plan I created to outline the buying process for a software platform. Note the Starter Kit resources in parentheses that I can provide at specific stages in this process:

- Form the evaluation team
- Kick off the project

- Define the scope of your project and begin document best practices (Deployment Roadmap)
- Define initial filter criteria
- Screen and identify potential options
- Develop evaluation criteria (Requirements List)
- Identify preferred options
- Develop business case for investment (ROI calculator, case studies)
- Select a vendor and negotiate terms
- Sign the contract

Once you and the prospect agree on this plan, you can gain critical intelligence into their buying process. Who are the stakeholders and decision-makers? Who owns the budget, and what kind of business case is required to secure funds? How does the procurement process work? As you answer these questions, create a timeline for each step and assign completion dates. Similar to a close plan *(***Technique #22: Plan to Close with a Close Plan***)*, the Evaluation Plan will put you in a much better position to forecast your deal and drive it to closure.

Deployment Roadmap

The Deployment Roadmap includes the factors and best practices a prospect needs to consider to ensure a speedy and successful deployment. For example, you might compare a "fast start" deployment to an "all-in" approach that requires more investment and resources. The Roadmap will help scope out your deal and press the prospect to make choices about their desired path. Bringing these options to a prospect's attention early in the process enables them to debate the pros and cons of each approach before making decisions.

An additional benefit of the Roadmap is that it changes the prospect's mindset from *"Do I buy?"* to *"How can I be successful?"* Every salesperson knows that it's a good thing when the prospect stops asking "if" and begins asking "how" and this is one more way that you can draw the prospect in and position yourself as the frontrunner.

ROI Calculator

Today, every major purchase needs to be backed by a strong business case. The ROI Calculator helps the prospect to quantify the benefits of your product by applying their own data to produce a speculative return. It's usually a spreadsheet into which the prospect inputs several variables and—Voila!—a clear calculation of the financial benefits they can expect from working with you.

If you're lucky, your company has already developed an ROI Calculator. If not, create your own and get your manager's blessing to offer it to prospects. Considering that your buyers need to present a clear and measurable ROI as part of their business case, the creation of an ROI calculator is a worthwhile investment that will help you and your clients.

Targeted Case Studies

Customer case studies are the easiest item on this list because every company wants to showcase its customer successes. Your Marketing group has likely created many of these, and they're often posted on the website. Not only do customer stories build your credibility, they can also be used as a proxy to understand financial benefits if you don't have an ROI Calculator. Find success stories that closely mirror your prospect's own business needs and market, and use these to open the door for reference calls to seal the deal.

* SHOWTIME *

Since your intent is to influence the buyer as early as possible in the process, offer the Starter Kit as soon as you've qualified them as a valid prospect. Don't wait for your competition to write the rulebook; seize the initiative and take the lead with your buyer. Your Starter Kit becomes a valuable tool for trial closes as well; prospects that accept your offer to help can be considered more likely to buy from you, and therefore forecast with more confidence.

Asking the right discovery questions is key to uncovering which elements of the Starter Kit could be helpful for the prospect. Make a point to ask these questions on your first discovery call:

- *Have you defined your requirements yet, and can you share them with me?* If requirements are vague, I introduce my Requirements List and my requirements become their requirements.
- *Have you bought solutions like mine before?* If they have, they'll be able to walk me through the evaluation and procurement process. If not, I share the Evaluation Plan and work with them to establish dates for each step.
- *Would it be helpful to share our experience deploying our product with several customers and highlight some of the choices you'll need to make?* This opens the door to sharing the Deployment Plan and customer case studies.
- *What kind of an internal business case do you need to present for this purchase?* This is the perfect opening to introduce both the ROI Calculator and case studies and begin building a bulletproof business case for your product.
- *Is there a formal process and evaluation team in place?* A defined process and assigned team are good signs that indicate they're serious about a purchase.

Rather than just attaching your Starter Kit documents to an email and sending it along, schedule time with the prospect to walk them through the details. I'll set up a call to review the Requirements List with the buyer, or help them to input their data into the ROI calculator. The key is helping them to understand the value of each resource and making it easy for them to use.

Once you've helped the prospect build some structure and gain confidence in your ability to help them, it's time to give them a push. You want more commitment, and this might involve writing a Close Plan together, introducing key executives, or beginning conversations with Procurement and Legal. *So, you want to develop initial filter criteria by May and begin evaluating vendor options by June. Why don't we look at June 15 for an onsite demonstration with your entire team? Can we ask your SVP to attend?* At this point, you've built credibility and established yourself as the lead vendor, and the prospect should have no problem taking the next step in the process with you.

Rewrite the Rulebook helps you to accomplish a number of important goals. You're demonstrating your expertise and thought leadership. You're presenting an organized approach to the buying process that gives the prospect more confidence in your ability to deliver for them. You're positioning yourself as the frontrunner and shutting out the competition.

When you've written the rulebook, there's an air of quiet certainty on both sides as you guide the customer along the path to a sale. Your destination: a signed contract, new relationship, and new customer. When you leave the conventional sales cycle behind to write the rules in your favor, you won't just win—you'll *own* the game.

Sales "rock stars" challenge conventions, question everything, reframe problems, take measured risks, and experiment often. In today's business environment, the innovative sales rep should be the standard, not the exception. The pace at which business moves demands agility—not a dogmatic adherence to rules and process, which only slow you down. I'm not advocating total rebellion against the system—you want to keep your job—but rather a willingness to step outside the corporate structure and think differently. As the goal of innovation is to drive even better results by trying new things, you should see a measurable improvement in customer satisfaction, deals closed and revenue booked. No sales manager will question your methods if you're delivering revenue, and you'll be given all the creative space you need.

Steve Jobs once said, "Innovation distinguishes between a leader and a follower." When you look at your own organization, you know who the innovators are because they're often the trailblazers whose ideas are quickly adopted by the rest of the salesforce. To them, nothing is sacred, and everything is negotiable. They'll tear up the price sheet and propose outrageous payment terms if it's the right move to close a deal. They present creative solutions to help their customers. They ask lots of questions, and listen more than they speak. They succeed; they fail; and they're not afraid of either outcome. Give me a team of these people and I guarantee I'll be able to sell anything to anybody, at any price point. Why? **Because this team will figure out the right model and make it work.**

Many of you might have trouble locating a single creative bone in your body. That's OK, because **innovation is an attitude, a skill, and a muscle that can be developed.** To become an innovative salesperson, you'll need to overcome the personal and organizational limits that may be hindering your growth. Your company may not make it easy for you either; many organizations punish unconventional thinking instead of encouraging it. Step outside the line one too many times and you'll get squashed. I get it; nobody said innovation was easy. If it were, we'd all be innovators. It requires effort, practice, courage, and a willingness to try and fail.

There are opportunities to innovate in everything you do: prospecting, process, proposals, pitching, closing, reporting, customer service, and communications. While most of us are good at learning and following the rules (it's how we survive), a few leaders find massive success by swimming against the tide. The spirit of innovation is what separates the thought leaders from the order-takers, and the more you flex your creative muscles, the stronger they'll become.

* GAME PREP *

Contrary to popular perception, most visionaries don't sit around waiting for the thunderbolt to strike. Rather, they know three absolute truths about innovation: (1) it can be learned, (2) it takes time, and (3) it can be improved with practice. Many organizations use techniques proven to stimulate creative thinking, and I'll share some of these with you in ***Showtime***. Over time and with constant application, your ability to transcend conventional thinking and look at problems through a different lens like Richard Feynman will become less of an effort than a reflex.

A good place to start is to examine your own attitude towards innovation. Do you follow the rules, or are your comfortable stepping over the line? How do you feel about failure? Do you dare to be different, or go-along-to-get-along? Be honest with yourself, because a self-assessment will establish your start point and determine the steepness of your climb.

Next, examine your past performance. What examples can you think of when you thought differently or ignored the rules? Can you name a situation in which you were innovative? If you can cite multiple examples, your spirit of innovation is strong and you're already on your way. But if you're struggling to remember even one example, you have your work cut out for you. Don't let the challenge dissuade you; innovation is always possible, and with a conscious effort to improve and apply new thinking, you'll see results.

I mentioned earlier the personal and institutional limits that can prevent you from being more creative in your sales role. Once you've assessed your attitude towards innovation, consider your company and the environment in which you operate. Does your organization give you latitude to maneuver, or are there strict protocols in place? Is innovation encouraged or crushed? How does your manager feel about trying a new approach? Because this person is often your first line of approval, it's in your interest to get him/her on board. The most effective way to do this is to present your proposal in terms of what's best for the customer:

> *"Juanita, ABC Corp. is ready to buy, but they have a unique situation with the user community that our current licensing structure won't accommodate. I have some ideas on how we can better meet their needs and push them to buy now, and I'd like to review these with you."*

A good manager will give you space to try new things; a *great* manager will give you a "failure MBO"[2] that measures how many times you tried and failed. Success is great, but failure indicates that you're trying new things, and this is positive. When new ideas work, you drive better results. When they fail, you learn from it, adjust, and move on. This constant cycle of experimentation, assessment and adjustment is what the very best innovators do— from visionaries to inventors to corporate R&D groups.

There *is* creativity in sales, and here are just a few examples where you can be more imaginative and resourceful in your approach:

- Prospecting
- Phone and email communications
- Sales pitch
- Presentation style
- Sales process
- Problem-solving
- Solution creation
- Deal terms
- Closing

---

[2] MBO = Management by Objective; the goals that managers assign to measure an employee's progress

- Account management
- Customer upsell

* SHOWTIME *

By its nature, innovation is an attitude; a process; a different way of thinking and solving problems. Below are several concepts and techniques that should aid you in your journey toward becoming a more innovative sales rep:

Failing Forward

This concept was captured in a quote from Thomas Edison when he was asked how he felt about repeatedly failing to design a working light bulb: "I have not failed. I've just found 10,000 ways that won't work."

One of my customers shared his annual performance report with me. To my surprise, I saw that in addition to his achievements, he was also being measured by the number of times he had failed. "If I'm not failing," he told me, "I'm not trying enough new things."

Accepting failure is one of the most difficult and important steps towards becoming an innovator, because without failure there is no progress. True innovators regard failure as a learning opportunity that draws them one step closer to success. When you do fail, make sure you're failing forward.

Collaboration

I took the "Speed Dating" [for singles] concept and converted it into a regular activity at my quarterly sales meetings. Each salesperson would create a poster with details about one of their pending deals, including client background, business pain, and the solution they were proposing. Attendees would move from station to station and spend seven minutes brainstorming with each salesperson before moving on to the next station and repeating the process. By inviting input from a diverse group, each salesperson would generate a wealth of creative ideas that could be presented back to their clients. When we assessed the results, many of the ideas became game-changers that led to new deals and business.

Don't feel as though the entire burden of creativity rests solely on your shoulders. Collaboration with others can open a richness of ideas and dialogue. Whether it's designing a proposal, formulating strategies to upsell clients, or simply brainstorming novel ways to delight your customers, engage your colleagues whenever you can. You may be surprised at their creativity and willingness to help.

Ask Better Questions

My former CEO was fond of saying that finding answers was not really that hard; **the real challenge is asking the right questions**. You put yourself in the right position to exceed customer expectations when you have a comprehensive understanding of their business and the problems they're trying to solve. This can only come about by deep discovery with the customer and making sure that you ask the right questions.

I've built a discovery template with more than 100 questions, and I choose 15 to 20 of these when I'm interviewing a new prospect. I often see reps hurry through the discovery process because they want to accelerate their sales cycle, but they're doing themselves (and the client) a great disservice. If your customer knowledge is thin, you're likely to take down the first transaction that appears. When you really understand the customer's business, you can bring big ideas to the table and present more creative solutions. Learn to operate at this level and significant financial and professional rewards will follow.

Experimentation

Multiple studies of innovative people have revealed an interesting fact: they aren't wild risk-takers who throw caution to the wind and plunge headlong into questionable endeavors. Instead, they take **measured** risks, and use experimentation to validate what their instincts are telling them. *Fail fast, fail smart* is a mantra in the business world today, and it gives people the latitude to try new things—and even fail—as long as they learn from the experience and apply these lessons wisely. One of my clients even maintained a knowledge base of their experiments and failures so that employees could see what their predecessors had learned before undertaking a new course of action.

Commit to trying one new thing every week and document what you've learned. With this knowledge, plot your next move. Great ideas don't usually drop from the sky, but instead result from a deliberate process. When you find something that works, keep doing it. If you fail, try to understand the reasons why, and reroute your efforts in a different direction.

The Power of Observation

Quick—what's the first thought that pops into your head when I mention Benjamin Franklin?

If your answer is that he invented electricity, you're not alone, but you're also not correct. Benjamin Franklin did *not* invent electricity; he ran experiments to observe how electricity *acted* (the famous kite), and developed insights that eventually led to the invention of our vast electrical infrastructure and countless electric devices. His process was to assemble clues and evidence, run experiments to validate his hunches, and eventually develop theories that could be tested and proven.

Salespeople need to keep their eyes open and improve their powers of observation. Because we're on the front line of business, we're in a unique position to see what's happening in the market and with our clients. Just like Benjamin Franklin, make a point to notice clues, develop hunches and test your own theories. You'll see opportunities that nobody else does, and more importantly, figure out how you can benefit from them.

#3: Three New Ideas

Winners bring big, bold ideas to the table and passionately advocate for them. Once you've closed the blockbuster deals, you'll never settle for small deals again.

"Surveys of customers consistently show that they put the highest value on salespeople who make them think, who bring new ideas, who find creative and innovative ways to help the customer's business."
- Excerpt from *The Challenger Sale* by Matthew Dixon and Brent Adamson

The Solution Selling model teaches that deep discovery is the key to unlocking a customer's needs and mapping these needs to your solution. The fundamental assumption in this approach, of course, is that customers actually *know* what these needs are. Through experience, we know that this is not always the case. By contrast, the Challenger Selling model relies less on discovery than on developing a thorough knowledge of the customer's marketplace. You want to challenge the customer's thinking and core beliefs by offering novel solutions to their problems based on your deep understanding of their business. It's more about *telling* than *asking*, and Challenger Selling contends that the best way to engage the customer in meaningful conversation is to bring fresh ideas and perspective to the conversation. **Three New Ideas** is built on the same premise.

To execute this technique, you research your client's business, market, trends and competitors, and brainstorm to produce three groundbreaking ideas that you can pitch to the client. It takes work, but the results can be spectacular. It's audacious, unconventional, and often successful, because it opens up a provocative dialogue that will showcase your creativity and willingness to go the extra mile for your customers. **Three New Ideas** shines a whole new light on the customer's challenge and your ability to solve it, and the benefits of this approach are compelling:

- You direct the conversation in promising new directions;
- You increase your credibility as a strategic partner (not just a vendor);
- You differentiate yourself from your competition; and
- You position high-value solutions to maximize your upside and potential return.

Let me give you an example. While employed by a startup selling crowdsourcing software, I'd been dancing with a prospect for almost a year. The prospect would show up for the calls and meetings, say all the right things, make noise about buying, and then disappear at the eleventh hour when it was time to make a commitment. Still, I felt something was there. I resolved to jumpstart the process by changing the dynamic, and **Three New Ideas** seemed like a perfect approach.

I studied the prospect's financials and press releases, and read all the articles I could find about their business. I pressed my contacts for inside information about the company, and asked what their executives were working on. I researched their competitors and read analyst's reports. Whenever I had an idea, I wrote it down in my notebook for further investigation. Within two weeks, I had several promising ideas that I could expand and refine. Since the entire premise of **Three New Ideas** is to introduce concepts that will result in a sale, I made sure that my software platform was a central component of every solution.

I sent an email titled "Three Great Ideas to Help Your Business" to the decision-makers. Without revealing the ideas themselves, I gave the executives a sneak peek at each idea to pique their curiosity and improve the chances that they'd take my call.

- Idea #1 would move the customer's core product farther upstream on the value chain.
- Idea #2 would improve execution by empowering each group with the information they needed to make speedy decisions.
- Idea #3 was building a system to solicit new ideas from remote employees.

While it can be helpful to solicit ideas and feedback from your contacts, *you want to make your pitch to the decision-makers*. Big, strategic ideas require sponsorship from someone with a strategic mindset and the influence to make things happen. Ask your contact for their help setting up this meeting, or send the executive an email that reveals just enough of your plan to get them interested. Try this: *"I've been researching your business, and I have a couple of exciting ideas to share with you, including one solution I believe will raise revenues by 30%. When could we find 20 minutes to discuss?"* Busy executives don't have time to chitchat, but new ideas that can make a big impact in their business will always grab their attention. Make your email stand out!

In terms of presenting your ideas, the pitch should include: (1) a problem statement, (2) your proposed solution, and (3) a plan for them to get started. Recall the earlier example of the three ideas I pitched to my client, in particular my idea about a system to solicit new ideas from employees. Through my research, I knew that remote employees felt disconnected from HQ, and there was rising concern among management about employees leaving the company. My pitch went something like this:

> *"For the past three months, we've been talking about providing you with a crowdsourcing platform to engage your employees and solicit good ideas. I understand your business is growing through acquisitions, and that has presented cultural and employee retention challenges. Here's my idea: use my platform to solicit suggestions from your remote employees about how you can make them feel more connected to the rest of the company. You'll acknowledge their concerns, give them a voice, and make them part of the solution. If we get started in the next two weeks, you can run your first campaign within 30 days."*

My customer loved the idea. If I were less proactive, I would have pursued a more vague line of inquiry, like *"I hear your acquisitions are running into trouble. Tell me more about this. What do you think we could do about it?"* Instead, I used my insight to propose an idea that I believed to be a winner, and gave them a reason to get started right away. Executives are hard to pin down, so always ASK (**#18: ASK for the Business**) for the business once you've pitched your ideas. When the customer accepts, make sure you've defined a clear plan of action to help them get started. This shows foresight and preparation on your part, and gives everyone the confidence they need to push forward with a purchase.

One salesperson I taught this technique to shared the following story: he had come across an article about an innovative promotion being run by Starbucks. Borrowing several ideas from this promotion, he typed up an email and sent it to his marketing contacts at competing coffee companies. More than half of them called back wanting to know more about his idea and how he could help. If you're selling to vertical markets, it's fair to assume that all of the companies in this space share similar challenges. In this case, the rep seized on a good idea and took the initiative with Starbucks' competitors. I love this application of **Three New Ideas** to open doors with new prospects, and it illustrates how techniques like this one can evolve when wielded by capable and motivated salespeople.

What if the prospect rejects all of your ideas? There are no guarantees in business, so this is certainly a possibility. If it happens, simply go back to the drawing board and come up with more ideas. Keep at it until *something* sticks or you decide that this prospect isn't a good target and move on. The point is that everyone welcomes new ideas, and it can't hurt your reputation (or your bank balance) to become known as the salesperson who goes the extra mile for their customers and *always* brings new ideas to the table.

#4: Go Looking for Trouble

Companies in trouble need help—fast. Their urgency can become your opportunity if you know how and where to go looking for trouble.

In the midst of the 2013 holiday shopping season, hackers stole credit and debit-card information from 40 million Target shoppers. A few weeks later, Target revealed that email, mailing addresses and other personal information had also been compromised in the hack, and the total number of shoppers exposed was actually closer to 70 million. Target took a substantial hit to its revenue as a result of this breach, a devastating blow from which it has yet to fully recover.[3]

A year later, hackers penetrated the servers at JPMorgan Chase, stealing several gigabytes of data, including checking and savings-account information. As expected, this act of theft was a major hit to the company's image and reputation. Moreover, it happened despite the fact that JPM spent $250 million on cybersecurity in 2014 with roughly 1,000 employees focused solely on preventing this type of attack.[4]

Now, picture yourself as a sales rep for a cybersecurity software firm during this period. *Target and JPM's nightmare would have been your dream.* Personally, I'd have been on the phone to the heads of Security and IT at these companies *the very next day.* These two companies are examples of the unfettered sales opportunity known as **the company in trouble**.

A variety of events can strike corporate America with the velocity and destructiveness of a meteorite: security breaches; corporate malfeasance; missed earnings; major product misses or recalls; disruption by a new technology or competitor; the list goes on and

---

[3] Source: http://www.nytimes.com/2014/03/14/business/target-missed-signs-of-a-data-breach.html&_r=0low

[4] Source: http://www.cbsnews.com/news/why-250m-didnt-protect-jp-morgan-from-hackers/

on. If a troubled company believes that it can spend its way out of trouble, it will divert people, resources and cash to fix the problem. This is a golden opportunity for the right vendor, and if you go looking for trouble, that vendor can be you.

It's important to keep your antennae up and be prepared when the right type of situation presents itself. Cybersecurity sales reps must have been lined up around the block at Target and JPM after the news broke. Both companies probably spent millions of dollars to address their problems. Can an organization buy back its reputation and renew customer confidence after this kind of breach? It's hard to say, but that won't stop a company from madly overspending to mitigate their damages. You don't need to monitor the business newswires 24/7 to find these opportunities either, because *companies in trouble are just as likely to come calling on you.* You can only imagine the head of JPMorgan's security group pulling his/her team together and telling them, "Cost is no object. Bring me the best partners to solve this problem. We need to make sure this never happens again."

I've had prospects in full-panic mode contact me before I knew how acute their pain really was. As I began to research their company, I'd turn up a news article that clued me into the severity of their situation, and suddenly the real picture would begin to materialize. The telltale signs were all there: the urgency in their tone; a desire to skip ahead in the sales cycle and discuss a purchase immediately; the presence of executives who would normally delegate this work; little or no pushback on pricing; and muzzling the attack dogs in Legal and Procurement. Fear is a powerful motivator, and it's never pretty when people are feeling the weight of an entire company bearing down on them as they struggle to right the ship.

This technique is *not* about profiting from the misfortune of others, but rather presenting the right solution at the right time to help companies that desperately need your help. Salespeople are not mercenaries, but we *are* opportunists, and the company in trouble can present a massive opportunity. When your product works in the way it was intended, you become part of the solution. It's a good feeling when you know that you helped the customer turn their fortunes around and probably saved some jobs as well. Plus, you'll have a loyal customer for life.

* GAME PREP *

You should always be on the lookout for the company in trouble. Start by reading the business news daily and looking for telltale signs. Here are a couple of recent headlines that I pulled from the newswire:

- "Wells Fargo fined \$185M for fake accounts; 5,300 were fired" (USA Today 9/9/16)
- "Volkswagen, Audi accused of using software to cheat US diesel emissions tests" (CNET 9/18/15)
- "Caterpillar Cuts Jobs, Revenue Outlook: Equipment maker projects 10,000 job cuts, revenue falling for record fourth-straight year" (WSJ 9/24/15)
- "Biogen to cut workforce" (WSJ 10/21/15)

Headlines like these indicate companies in trouble, and depending on the products you sell, can represent business opportunities for you. Set up four or five automated newsfeeds that can push targeted information out to you, and make a point to browse the business section each morning while sipping your coffee. You're looking for bad news, and the following events can reveal a company in trouble:

- Restructuring, especially downsizing
- Sub-par earnings announcements
- Changes in the leadership team
- Hacking and/or security breaches
- Corporate malfeasance
- Closing offices/locations
- Bankruptcy (Chapter 7, not Chapter 11)
- Job cuts and layoffs
- Acquisition rumors
- Product recall or failure
- New competitors or major disruptions in the market
- New or pending legislation and regulations

In addition to specific events, keep your eye on industry and market trends. If gas prices are plunging, it's a good bet that oil and gas companies are scrambling to replace lost revenue. The sales rep whose products address this challenge can target the top 20 oil companies and start calling. Understanding trends and the bigger picture will help you to anticipate which companies could use your help, maybe even *before* they think they need it. It can never hurt to be the first one there, and anticipating demand gives you a big advantage over the competition.

An intimate knowledge of your value proposition and the major business problems your product solves is critical to preparing your approach. You can't cure everyone's pain, so focus on situations in which you *know* that you can be the hero. The cybersecurity firm helping Target to prevent a future data breach is an obvious example, and consider others that apply to your own business. Always keep your antennae extended for the right companies, events, and situations, and run (don't walk) to the phone when they present themselves.

One trap to avoid: it's easy to be distracted by a free-falling stock price, but remember—the stock market is both fickle and driven by its own rules. Companies may spend over the long-term to drive up their stock price, but you'll see more immediate opportunities with organizations that have exposed a fundamental weakness in their business or suffered a calamitous event. Falling stock prices can be signs of bigger problems, but are not always indicative of a company in trouble.

* SHOWTIME *

When you find the company in trouble, your first task is to identify and understand the problem. This knowledge will help you to devise a strategy and move quickly with your solution. Confidence is important—and contagious—so you need to make the prospect believe you're the answer to their prayers. Be acutely aware that companies in trouble are often sensitive about their plight, which might be playing out on the front page of the business news.

Pursue this opportunity with the appropriate tact and express your willingness to help.

If we put ourselves in the shoes of the cybersecurity sales rep calling Target HQ, the conversation might go something like this:

> *"I read about your recent security issues, and these are exactly the kind of threats that we've helped companies like Sears and Kohl's protect against. Working together, we can make sure that you're fully protected against future breaches. Let's find a time this week to speak, and I'll show you exactly how I can help you."*

Don't dance around the elephant in the room; instead make it central to your messaging and value proposition. Remember, unless they reach out to you, a cold call to a company in trouble *is still a cold call*. The surest way to guarantee a callback is to let them know that you're an expert at solving their problem and that you want to help.

Once you're engaged, expect a shortened discovery process because (1) it's not needed, and (2) companies in trouble are looking for answers and fast action, not an extended sales cycle. In a way, it's a dream-selling scenario, because these prospects will move with *urgency*. If you can't match their pace, they'll find someone who can. Get your manager to help you clear internal roadblocks and red tape if your company is large and not naturally built for speed.

Companies in trouble move with urgency and determination because their very survival can depend on finding and implementing the right solution. They'll be spending money with *someone*, and this someone can be you if you make it a point to **Go Looking for Trouble**.

#5: Read the Tea Leaves

Change happens whether you welcome it or dread it. Smart salespeople try to anticipate the future and think about how they can create opportunity in a shifting business landscape.

"It is not the strongest or the most intelligent who will survive but those who can best manage change."
- Leon C. Megginson, Ph.D, Professor and Author

It's been said that the only constant in life is change, and it's easy to recall many businesses that failed to navigate through the turbulent waters of a shifting marketplace and paid a steep price. *Yahoo! Blockbuster. RIM.* In this age of disruption and hyper-competition, companies strive to be agile and adaptable; they need to keep up with big competitors and the yet-unknown startups that break all the rules and steal their market share before anyone can react. The pace of business seems to accelerate every day, and salespeople are compelled to either embrace this new velocity or become a casualty of it.

We roll with the punches as priorities shift, organizations change, and people come and go. We close our deals and do just fine, but even greater opportunities await us. I'm a surfer, so here's a surfing analogy: you can float in the line-up alongside everyone else and catch some decent rides, but the really gnarly waves are farther out where few dare to paddle. To ride these monsters, you need to look beyond the swells in front of you and anticipate what's coming behind them. In this way, you'll be prepared to catch the biggest wave and the ride of your life.

In the business world, this means looking for signs of change, anticipating how the change will affect you, and looking for ways to turn it to your advantage.

I had the dubious honor of calling all my customers to let them know that my company was going to raise our prices in the new fiscal year, which was only four short weeks away. Instead of

45

approaching this task like a walk to the gallows (which is how I felt), I tried to find the upside in the situation. When I spoke with customers, I would point out that they could still make purchases at the current pricing levels for another month. The cursed price hike turned into a blessing: I was able to prompt several companies to buy now and pull forward $86,000 in sales.

Price increases are an excellent example of how change can drive opportunity. Big companies alter their pricing with impunity. The act is usually driven by the notion that "we can make more money" by tweaking the pricing model, and the profit motive virtually guarantees that new pricing will *not* benefit the customer. Consider my example: any customers contemplating buying new products would pay a higher price if they delayed their decision. The looming price increase created a sense of urgency that turned a negative (having to deliver bad news) into a positive (closing $86K in revenue).

This is the essence of **Read the Tea Leaves**. You must be an opportunist to excel in sales, because timing really is everything. **It's up to you to anticipate shifts in pricing, personnel, organization, business models, markets, and other conditions, and figure out how best to monetize these changes.** Here are several examples of events that can offer revenue possibilities for prescient sales reps skilled at predicting the future:

- **Price increases:** If a price hike is on the horizon, it's standard practice to notify your customers and give them time to adjust. Per my earlier example, customers deliberating a purchase have more incentive to buy now than wait and pay a premium later.
- **New pricing model:** Your organization makes big changes to its pricing structure and how customers are charged. One of my employers changed its software licensing metric from "per-seat" to "per-CPU" and this helped me deliver an exceptional quarter by auditing existing customers and bringing them into compliance with the new standard.
- **New product launches:** Many organizations will offer incentives to drive initial sales of a new product. The sales

department should be at the forefront of every new product introduction.

- **Organizational changes:** Executive shake-ups, changes to support policies, and divisions being sold or acquired are all examples of routine organizational changes at your company that may affect your customers. Your challenge is to figure out the specific impact on each customer and present a plan to guide them through these changes with minimal disruption.

And lest we forget…

- **Customer change:** It's likely that your customer's business is changing as rapidly as yours, and these changes can also bring about new opportunities. Your customer acquires another company and doubles their user count. You learn that a new competitor is disrupting your customer's market. An employee about to retire wants to cement their legacy with a signature program. Your champion knows that her management team is going to change and wants to lock-in your contract while she still has the authority. Each of these is a real-life example from my own sales career, and each time I was able to anticipate these changes and turn them to my advantage. The more tuned-in you are to your customer's business, the likelier you are to find ways to benefit from the inevitability of change.

* GAME PREP *

Information is power, and it's also the key to succeeding with **Read the Tea Leaves**. You want to get ahead of events rather than just react to them, but you don't need to be a fortune-teller to do so. *You just look for the clues.* To anticipate change in your company, you need to keep your eyes and ears open, talk to others, and plant a bug in the executive suite. If you're not in senior leadership and therefore privy to conversations about strategy and direction, you can still develop your own "early warning system" by **volunteering to be the sales liaison with the management team**.

I played this role once and it meant sitting in on strategy and planning meetings with the executives as the sales team's representative. I provided sales perspective on what we were seeing in the market, and communicated messages from management to the team. Although the role was purely voluntary, it put me in a position to learn about pending changes before they happened *and* gave me time to plan my approach. If the sales liaison role doesn't exist at your company, volunteer to be the first. You'll show initiative, get to know the executives better, and put yourself in the right position to see the future before it happens.

Keeping yourself current with the latest news, developments, and inside information at your customer's organization is a bit more challenging. Setting up listening posts and early-warning systems are important. Start by scanning the headlines daily. I use Google Alerts and a custom Yahoo! dashboard that pushes relevant news directly to me. Keep an eye on the market and competitors as well, because larger trends can also impact your clients.

In parallel, work all of your contacts and press them for inside information and rumors that might foreshadow a change in their business. To do this, just call them up and let them talk. Employees are usually the first to know when something's cooking, and they can tip you off before this information becomes public (within all ethical boundaries, of course). **The more information you have, the better, so keep your antennae up and become an active listener.**

I was speaking with one of my contacts and she speculated on an upcoming merger. She mentioned that the acquiring company had already invested in a technology similar to mine, and this disclosure raised red flags for both of us. Her work with my product was a big part of her overall responsibility, and it wasn't hard to imagine that if my product was replaced, she might go with it. We decided on the spot to write up the paperwork that would extend her contract with my company for another two years, locking in this commitment while she still had the authority to approve the transaction.

This situation is a perfect example of how **Read the Tea Leaves** is meant to work. My contact tipped me off to an impending change, and her natural question was, *what does this mean for me?* Deciding that the impact could be negative, we collaborated to take steps that met both of our interests: I booked an unexpected 2-year contract extension, and she bought herself some job security. Rather than leaving ourselves at the mercy of change, we seized the initiative and wrote our own script for the future.

* SHOWTIME *

When you become aware of a shift in circumstances that might portend an opportunity, your work begins. **You need to understand the implications of an event, its impact on you, and how it might lead to an opportunity.** For example, if you find out that your customer is acquiring a competitor, you know this means more users and license fees. If your customer is *being* acquired, experience tells us to expect shifts in strategy, direction and personnel. Accordingly, you may want to take steps to protect your turf. There's a huge increase in corporate M&A activity today. Mergers mean new users and growing your product footprint. If your customer is being acquired, consider both threats to your existing business *and* new opportunities to grow.

In your own organization, the most relevant changes will involve pricing, the introduction of new product lines, shifts in strategy, and organizational changes. Events like price increases are easy; you want to push wavering customers to buy now before their costs go up. New product launches are perfect for promotions that offer price breaks to early adopters. New people present an opportunity to set up F2F meetings with clients and make an introduction. Always look for the upside and the opportunity in every changing circumstance, and you'll stay two steps ahead of your colleagues and competition.

History (and Darwin) has shown that adaptability is key to survival, and this is certainly true for companies and salespeople. Look toward the future and **Read the Tea Leaves** to anticipate what's coming. You'll be better prepared to overcome potential challenges and create new opportunities.

#6: New Faces

It's frustrating when your deal is stuck. Bringing in the right people at the right time can be exactly what you need to get your deal back on track and win the business.

I can recall one deal in my pipeline that I had been forecasting for 186 days. I remember the exact length of time because my sales manager would run a "Days in Pipe" report, and ask reps to justify any deals that were older than 100 days. He believed (not unreasonably) that if we couldn't provide a clear path to close a deal after three months, the deal should be removed from the forecast. This particular deal was becoming a running joke, as my manager would keep bringing it up and I would keep insisting that it would close with. . . just. . . a. . . little . . . more . . . time.

This deal was languishing in forecasting hell because my prospect had recently gone through a reorganization, which killed our momentum. The sponsor liked us and was convinced we were the right solution, but he couldn't pull the trigger without the blessing of his new SVP. As fate would have it, the SVP was flying around the world meeting teams and completely unaware of our project. As a result, my deal continued to bump along, quarter after quarter, while the sponsor tried desperately to get the SVP's attention and secure his approval.

Deciding to do something that I should've done a long time ago, I approached my EVP and asked for his help. He placed a call to the SVP and scheduled a time to talk. Their call went well, and my EVP was able to convince their SVP that this project was important and worthy of his support. After making internal inquiries, the SVP signed the deal. I won't ever forget the look on my manager's face when I showed him the contract; it almost made up for the months of torment I'd endured.

Another example: one of my employers had just hired a new CEO. When he arrived, he asked me to set up meetings with all my existing customers and important prospects. I must have scheduled ten meetings in those first two months, and I came away from this sprint with a $300K deal and almost $500K in sales pipeline. What happened? The CEO met with senior decision-makers and pitched a brand-new kind of consulting that I didn't even know we offered. As it turned out, *he was making it all up*, but the customers loved it and somehow we figured out how to deliver on what he'd promised. I went on to have the best year of my entire career.

One final story: one of my larger deals was languishing in the fiery pits of IT purgatory for several months. The IT stakeholders were being unreasonable and taking their sweet time on a security review that they'd demanded from my company. Their people skills were devilishly terrible; one of them actually said to me, *"What the hell do you know? You're just a salesguy!"* Since my sponsors were unable (or unwilling) to take them on, in desperation I turned to my CTO. He volunteered to go onsite with the customer—at our expense—and work side-by-side with them to complete the security audit. We both traveled to their office, and my CTO literally disappeared for two days. He didn't respond to calls or messages, and nobody knew where he was. When he re-emerged, we had secured the technical sign-off. The IT people, it turned out, loved him, and took him out to dinner every night he was in town! With the CTO's help and intervention, my deal closed two weeks later.

What's the common thread in these stories? Each time, the introduction of a new and strategically important player into the sales cycle was instrumental in changing the dynamics of the deal in a positive way. Whether you're looking to generate new business, resuscitate a deal, or push recalcitrant prospects to sign, **New Faces** is all about introducing the *right* person at the *right* time to drive a better outcome. It's a tried-and-true approach that works when you're facing challenges that we salespeople know only too well:

- Appearance of a new executive
- Technical challenges
- Stuck with low-level contact; no access to power
- Customer has no sense of urgency to buy
- Obstinate individuals or departments

- Deals shelved due to higher priorities
- Perception that your product is a "nice-to-have," not a priority
- Organizational lethargy and/or inefficiencies
- Organizational changes

Your first step toward successfully deploying this technique is to understand the people in your extended organization and the unique skills they can bring to the sales effort. Your second step is to correctly diagnose the situation with the prospect and match needs to the appropriate resource. Third, you need to be able to influence the outcome. Some companies are simply resistant to outside forces and will not respond to any of your best efforts. In this case, you need to decide whether you want to hang in there or move on to greener pastures. Finally, make the introduction and let your new player work their magic.

It's important to make a realistic assessment of your deal's close potential before introducing key personnel into the sales cycle. **New Faces** represents a doubling-down on your investment in a client, so this decision should never be made lightly. The wrong call makes you look bad, wastes everyone's time and carries an opportunity cost as people are diverted from more important work. This is especially true if you're asking an executive for help. On the other hand, skillful application of this technique takes full advantage of the people and resources available to you. When you're in a competitive sales cycle and all other things are basically equal, your people will make the difference and win you the business. **New Faces** is about solving problems, but it's also an opportunity to showcase your deep bench of expertise and talent.

It's funny: many executives want to earn bragging rights as sales "closers," and they relish the thought of getting hands-on in the sales cycle. To make the pot even sweeter, I've split my commission checks with people on my extended team and bought gifts and dinners to show my appreciation. It's a small price to pay compared to the impact these people have on my deals, and ensures that they'll continue to support me on future deals.

* GAME PREP *

Your first step is to recognize the people in your organization who are willing and able to help you in the sales effort. I'd include most of the executive team on this list, because good leaders know that nothing is more important than bringing in revenue. The CEO is your heaviest hitter—the "nuclear option," if you will—and should be called upon for VIP clients and very large deals. In smaller companies, the Founder can also function in this capacity. Many CEOs are extremely hands-on and love to spend time in front of customers, and this works to your advantage. The Head of Sales will be your go-to executive in most cases, and this individual should be ready to jump on a plane anywhere, anytime to help you close business.

When specific domain expertise is required, the CTO, CIO, or subject-matter experts are your best bet. Get to know this extended sales team along with their areas of expertise, strengths, weaknesses, demeanor with customers, and willingness to take direction from you (important). Once you begin working with colleagues in a live customer environment, you'll have a much better sense of how they operate and handle themselves, and this will influence your personnel decisions.

Consider your role as coach and quarterback. Your people need to be coached on the specifics of the deal and the role you expect them to play. I often type up a one-page opportunity synopsis that summarizes the deal, people, and outcomes I'm looking to achieve. Once they're up to speed, introduce this person to the prospect and manage them like you would any other team member. This means holding them accountable for results. As the quarterback, it's your play to call, but you also depend on their professionalism to get the job done. Remember that YOU own the client relationship and have the final say on any decisions affecting your client and your deal. This holds true whether you bring in the CEO or a sales engineer to help you.

While new people can be called upon to help you generate new business and pipeline—as was the case with my CEO story—the "stuck" deal is the most common scenario for this technique. Let's explore how **New Faces** can be used most effectively to "unstick" your stuck deals.

Stuck Deals

I'd characterize stuck deals as those that have stalled, regressed, or seem to be spiraling out of your control. It's an opportune time to rethink and modify your approach, and **New Faces** is often used to save deals that are slipping from *committed* to *lost.* You may need to move fast, so it's important to formulate your plan and introduce the right degree of urgency to the team.

New Faces is most effective when (1) the prospect has the means and desire to buy from you, (2) your solution is the right one for them, and (3) a new player can exert meaningful influence on the process and generate results. Avoid wasting valuable resources by throwing them against an immovable wall. For example, one of my deals became stuck in a prospect's completely inefficient procurement process. No amount of prodding or assistance from anyone in my company could change this, and it would've been a waste of time to try. I could only grind my teeth and ask my internal contact to do what he could to push the deal along.

Speaking of internal contacts, they're often as frustrated as you are when deals become stuck. They'll welcome new ideas and the introduction of new players to shift the dynamic. This is good, as you'll need their support to make the strategy work. They can feed you inside information, schedule meetings, and help you connect with the right people on their side. Their engagement will provide your new player with the information and access they need to get your stuck deal moving again.

* SHOWTIME *

Let's examine eight of the most common scenarios in which deals can become stuck, and assess how **New Faces** can be used to change the deal dynamic and drive your desired outcome:

1. **There's a new executive sponsor at the customer. You don't know this person, but she/he need to approve or fund your deal.**
   - Your ability to influence: High
   - Best course of action: Ask *your* executive to make a peer-to-peer connection with the new executive in order to build a relationship and ask for their support.

2. **You're stuck in a rut with a low-level contact, and don't have a relationship with the executive sponsor.**
   - Your ability to influence: High
   - Best course of action: Similar to #1, recruit your executive to reach out to his/her peer on the customer side and ask for help in moving the business forward. Your hands are clean and there's no appearance of making an end-run around your low-level contact.

3. **You have functional, technical or security challenges.**
   - Your ability to influence: High
   - Best course of action: This is exactly what your subject-matter experts are employed to do. Connect them with their counterparts on the prospect side, and don't let up until all outstanding issues are resolved to the prospect's satisfaction.

4. **The customer is taking forever in the sales cycle. This may be due to other priorities, organizational lethargy, or the need to follow an RFI/RFP process and investigate multiple vendors.**
   - Your ability to influence: Moderate
   - Best course of action: Consider new messaging at different levels in the buying organization. Occasionally I've asked my SVP to show up with a time-based incentive in his back pocket. But if a customer is forced to work through internal processes, it limits your ability to drive action.

5. **A specific individual or department is holding up your deal for personal or business reasons.**
   - Your ability to influence: Moderate

and lost based on their ability to address the underlying risks and fears that are masked by customer objections.

In other words, objections are just the tip of the iceberg; your true risk factors are usually hidden beneath the surface, and these must be revealed and dealt with before the buyer will sign the contract.

Some customers will share certain risk factors upfront, but most of them believe that their dirty laundry should not to be shared with vendors. What you get instead is a cover story, which is the agreed-upon version of the truth that buyers are willing to disclose to you. Considering that you plan your entire approach based on what the buyer has told you, it's important to cut through the cover story and understand what's truly going on. If your planning is based on incomplete or flawed intelligence, it's easy for you to start heading down the wrong path.

Your challenge is to: (1) move past the cover story to identify the risk factors, and then (2) minimize or eliminate these risks. When you eliminate risk, you take away the client's reasons *not to buy*. This is important, because deep down most people really do want to buy. They *need* new products and services to run their business. This works to your advantage, as long as you are strengthening the client's belief that there's more reward than risk in your transaction.

* GAME PREP *

Assume that every buyer has two stories: the cover story they're willing to share with you, and the *real* story that speaks to their internal deliberations, underlying fears, and perception of risk. It's not that the buyer is lying to you exactly, but instead choosing what facts to reveal and what facts to hold back. It's your job to keep questioning and poking at the cover story until you get a glimpse of the risk factors beneath. When they're revealed, you can formulate the best plan to eliminate them.

This work begins on day one with discovery. It pains me to say it, but most salespeople rush through the discovery process because they want to move customers into a sales cycle as quickly as possible. They buy the cover story and hope that it's true. *It's dangerous to simply accept the cover story without validating the facts for yourself.* A lack of persistence and vigor in the discovery process can lead to blind spots and "gotcha" scenarios in which supposedly committed deals fall through because you've failed to address the underlying risk.

Follow the Socratic method in your discovery process by designing a series of questions that will qualify your assumptions, challenge what you know, and get your client talking. Your goal is to penetrate the cover story (if it's not the real story) and draw out any critical risk factors that could jeopardize your deal.

As you move forward in the sales cycle, you should solicit and welcome objections from the buyer. Objections offer a glimpse of the bigger issues lurking below and provide clues for your investigation. If I'm the buyer, I don't tell my sales rep that I probably won't get budget approval to buy their product, or that my company's in financial distress. *Instead, I throw out an objection and tell them their product's too expensive.*

This is a classic objection, and you'll fail if you take it at face value. Objections should *not* be met with well-rehearsed responses, but instead with *more questions.* **Objections allude to fundamental issues of budget, authority, need, timeline, value and organizational structure, and all of these represent potential risk factors in your deal.** You don't need to "handle objections"; you need to search for the source of the objection and take steps to address it. This can only be achieved through vigorous and pointed questioning. You can explain why your pricing is actually quite reasonable until you're blue in the face, but if I can't afford to buy it, your wasting your time and mine.

If this concept shatters your perception of objection-handling, it's because most salespeople have been doing it wrong for years. Instead of probing deeper, they take cursory steps to overcome the objection and then express surprise when the customer walks: *I handled all their objections—why didn't they buy?* Roleplaying the objection-handling process is a common exercise in sales meetings, and this ritual needs to change. What the sales organization *should* be doing instead is training its salespeople to ask *better questions* and look for clues that expose the real risk factors.

Our more modern approach to objection-handling utilizes two of the sharpest tools from our sales toolbox: the **open-ended question** and **the trial close**. Let's review some common sales objections, speculate on what the customer might really be saying, consider the risk factors, and use open-ended questions and trial closes to discover the truth.

Objection #1

What the customer says: "Your product is too expensive."

What the customer may be thinking:
1. My boss needs to approve this purchase and he's giving me a hard time about it.
2. I've never spent this much money on a product before, and I'm nervous. If I make a bad decision, it could hurt my career.
3. I'm trying to fly under the radar and fit this into my budget. If I need to ask Finance for more money, their involvement could stretch this process out six months and I need your product now.

Possible underlying risk factors:
Budget, Authority, Need, Value

Smart follow-up questions:
- What's your budget approval process? Does your CFO or finance team need to approve?
- Are we within the approved budgetary limits? What happens if you need to find more money?
- Have you had a similar experience in the past buying products like mine?
- What kind of a business case do you need to present to justify this purchase? Can I help you prepare this story?
- What if we were to get the decision-maker on the phone and collaborate to work out a deal? Could you arrange this call?

Objection #2

What the customer says: "I'm happy with my current setup."

What the customer may be thinking:
1. You haven't presented a compelling-enough value proposition to convince me that I should buy.
2. I don't have the budget or authority to buy your product.
3. I'm content to just go along to get along. I don't want to rock the boat.

Possible underlying risk factors:
Budget, Authority, Need, Timeline, Value

Smart follow-up questions:
- What were the issues that prompted you to reach out to me in the first place?
- Have you already submitted a requisition for this purchase? And what happens to these funds if you don't buy?
- What's your vision of where you'd like to be next year? Can you get there *without making changes* to your current setup?
- Have I done a good job expressing my value proposition and what it means to you? If not, would you be willing to work with me to build a stronger business case?
- What if we were to run a pilot to test the concept?

Although you don't want to offend the prospect, your questioning needs to be relentless until you discover the truth. Sometimes this means just wearing your contact out until they relent and tell you what you want to know. In my examples, note that use of open-ended questions avoided Yes/No answers that didn't really explain anything. I've also used the trial close to compel the prospect to make an incremental commitment. This could be bringing in the decision-maker, or working with me to develop a business case. Prospects that commit and have actual skin in the game are more inclined to be transparent and honest with you.

The trial close in Objection #1 is to ask for a call with the decision-maker. **Nobody introduces the executive unless they're serious.** If a lack of executive support is your primary obstacle, the sponsor will schedule this call. Similarly, the trial close in Objection #2 is to work with the client to strengthen the business case or run a pilot. If the client is committed, they'll take me up on this. The most effective trial closes require some level of commitment from both parties, and it's a good sign if they're willing to make a parallel commitment to you.

If you're programmed to pull out your "objection-handling checklist", contrast your potential outcomes with those generated by my approach. You'll try to justify your pricing or convince the customer that they need to make a change, but you're failing to address the underlying risk factors. It may not happen right away, but you'll lose the deal. My approach is superior because it compels you to uncover the root cause of an objection and reveals the true risk factors that could kill a deal. Once you've formulated a plan to handle the risk, the customer simply runs out of reasons not to buy. They feel free and empowered to make a purchase.

* SHOWTIME *

At this point in the sales cycle, you've gotten to know the prospect fairly well. You've been through an upfront discovery process, held multiple conversations and meetings, and probed beneath the surface to identify possible risk factors that could jeopardize your deal. With a better understanding of the risk factors that the prospect is currently deliberating, you can initiate a course of action that will eliminate these risks and take away their reasons not to buy.

Recalling our two examples from ***Game Prep***, let's reveal what the prospect really meant when he/she raised an objection, and examine possible courses of action to eliminate the risk factors:

Objection #1: "Your product is too expensive."

What the customer really means:
Answer #1: My boss needs to approve this purchase and he's giving me a hard time.

Actions initiated:
- Confer with your sponsor about the executive's top priorities. Prepare a presentation framing your value proposition in terms that will resonate with the executive.
- Propose a meeting with the executive to present how your solution specifically addresses his priorities and will help him to achieve his goals.
- Set up a reference call between the executive and a satisfied client who has successfully solved the same problem.
- If needed, restructure the deal to ramp-up payments as the new customer's benefits are realized. But no offering discounts; that's what novice salespeople do.

Objection #2: "I'm happy with my current setup."

What the customer really means:
Answer #1: You haven't presented a compelling-enough value proposition to convince me that I should buy.

Actions initiated:
- Introduce tools like the ROI calculator and customer case studies to build a more complete business case.
- Ask your contact to sponsor a meeting with the executive to present your business case.
- Approach stakeholders to build a wider base of support.
- Initiate a trial allowing the prospect to try the product in a live setting to see its benefits firsthand.

When developing a proposal, you'll always find richness in collaborating with your extended sales team. Internal brainstorming sessions will give you a variety of viewpoints and angles with which to develop a response plan. Your goal is to come to the table with solutions that directly address the core issues and risk factors. The customer's willingness to work with you to reach a solution will be a good indicator of their intent, because **prospects who *want* to buy will work with you to eliminate their perceived risks.** If they resist your help, qualify them hard with trial closes to make sure they're serious buyers.

I can't overemphasize the importance of tearing down objections to reveal your prospect's real motivation and fears. I've seen many deals evaporate when salespeople fail to do this. In most cases, it comes as a nasty surprise, because everything appears to be going well and moving in the right direction. When salespeople sail through discovery, buy into the cover story, and mishandle objections, their forecasted deals will become—instead—ticking time bombs just waiting to go off.

To avoid this scenario, assume that *every* prospect's story is a cover story, and that *every* prospect is concealing underlying risks. Improve your discovery process and employ trial closes and open-ended questions to find the real risk factors, and then work hard to eliminate them. You'll win more often and avoid the nasty surprises that sneak up on salespeople who haven't yet learned the *right* way to handle buyer objections.

PART TWO

Build the Machine

"Welcome to the Machine."
- Pink Floyd, song title from 1975 album *Wish You Were Here*

Anyone who's spent time around salespeople has heard the term "sales machine," and it refers to the people, systems, resources, and processes that back up and perpetuate the sales effort. One of my most important mandates as a sales professional is to build this machine, and when it's operational it'll enhance and enable my sales effort. **The sole mission of the sales machine is to provide me with the support I need to close more deals and revenue.**

Too many salespeople burn out trying to shoulder the entire burden themselves—prospecting, deal advancement, closing, branding, networking, and content production. Building a vibrant sales machine is essential if you want to drive extraordinary results *and* remain sane.

There are many moving parts in the sales machine: the people on your executive and extended sales teams; systems like CRM and social media; resources like webinars and content production; and processes such as lead generation and RFP rapid-response. With your direction, this machine will supercharge your sales effort, create new opportunities, improve sales cycles, and ultimately generate more revenue. **Every top performer has a vibrant sales machine behind them, and it's your ticket to the top of the leaderboard and the President's Club penthouse.**

The 8 techniques presented in **Build the Machine** are:

#8: The Perfect Sale
Figure out who your ideal customers are, then go sell to them.

#9: Go Social
Salespeople need to be proficient with social media because it's where their buyers connect, work, talk, and relax. You can conquer this brave new world with a smart and savvy social-selling strategy.

#10: Get LinkedIn
LinkedIn is arguably the most important business-networking tool available to professionals today. Optimize your LinkedIn strategy to strengthen your brand and start conversations with more of the right people.

#11: The Art of the RFP
Although they're a ton of work, RFPs very often result in sales. By actively seeking out RFPs and building a quick-response effort, you can ensure that this effort pays off.

#12: Develop a Content Strategy
Fresh new content is the lifeblood of the Internet. If your goal is to capture an audience, build thought leadership, and give buyers a reason to engage with you, you need a self-sufficient content strategy.

#13: Build a Virtual Salesforce
If one salesperson can make 50 phone calls and talk to 5 people, how many prospects can 10 people talk to? Short of cloning yourself, building a virtual salesforce is your best bet to broadcast a powerful and far-reaching message.

#14: Open Your Customer's Little Black Book
Every referral or introduction a client makes on your behalf can be sales gold. Ask your clients to open their little black books and introduce you to their friends and colleagues. You'll boost your pipeline immediately and have even more conversations with receptive prospects.

#15: Run a Webinar
Internet broadcasting empowers you to deliver a targeted message and Call-to-Action to a large audience at a low cost. Increasingly, companies are realizing the power of the webinar and making it a key component of their customer outreach strategy.

#8: The Perfect Sale

Figure out who your ideal customers are, then go sell to them.

One exercise I always initiate with a new sales team is to develop or refine the Ideal Customer Profile ("ICP"). Also known as the *customer persona*, the ICP defines the characteristics of your "perfect customer": the company that potentially stands to realize the greatest benefit by adopting your solution. Once the ICP is defined, your marketing and sales teams can adjust their targeting efforts to ensure that resources are laser-focused on the companies most likely to buy from you. Although it sounds straightforward, I'm always amazed by how many people in an organization struggle to answer the question: *What companies are most likely to buy from us?*

The stakes are high. A failure to clearly define your ICP leads to misguided demand-generation efforts, a pipeline filled with long-shot prospects, low conversion rates, and disappointing sales results. On the other hand, companies that use the ICP as a guide can focus their resources on targeting the right prospects and transforming them into customers. As companies meeting the ICP criteria have a higher probability of becoming customers, deals and revenue can be forecast with more confidence. When you *know* that you're the right solution for a prospective client, it frees you up to be more proactive and assertive in the sales cycle.

The ICP is particularly useful in helping sales reps avoid one alluring trap that we all fall into at some point: **the white-hot prospect**. We all know this prospect: they show up out of nowhere, money in hand, threatening to buy. They push you to accelerate the sales cycle and demand pricing right away. Although they don't fit the mold of a typical customer, they're a very shiny object, and they eventually pull you in. You make them a priority and point your big guns in their direction, anticipating a fast sale and already dreaming about how you're going to spend your commission check.

The only problem is that when it's time to commit, they stop returning your calls. This goes on for several weeks, forcing you to make excuses to your manager and push what you thought was a sure thing out on your forecast. When you finally do connect with them, they tell you that there's a problem with the budget, or the executive has shifted everyone's attention to other priorities. The deal limps along for another month or two until, with great regret, you kill it in your pipeline, cursing the malevolent forces that sent the white-hot prospect your way.

With the ICP as your guide, you'll never fall into the white-hot prospect trap again, because you'll know that this company is an anomaly and needs to be treated with caution. Sales forecasting is about playing the odds, and your chances of closing a company outside of the ICP are not promising. **Prospects that don't meet your ICP need to be qualified hard, because the odds say that they won't become a customer.** The ICP acts as a filter that accelerates the process with qualified prospects, and signals danger with less-qualified companies. It's a gut-check for every prospect in your pipeline, and provides massive value by directing your valuable time and resources toward the prospects most likely to buy from you.

Of course, there are always exceptions. Not every company that buys will always fit neatly into the ICP profile. If you can check all the right boxes when qualifying a prospect in terms of pain, budget, and urgency, you should continue to work the deal. The primary value of the ICP is to establish a set of useful guidelines that will guide you as you handle inbound leads, build prospecting lists, work the deals in your pipeline, forecast deals, and decide where to invest your time to generate the best return.

* GAME PREP *

Whether you're developing the ICP from scratch or refining and validating a current definition, start with an analysis of your current customer base. Create a spreadsheet that lists "Customers" across one axis and "Criteria" across the other. Here's a list of possible ICP criteria:

- Industry or Vertical
- Revenue
- Buyer (role, level, and department)
- Profitability
- Geography
- # of employees
- Lifecycle (mature, growth, declining)
- Physical or technology infrastructure
- Public statements of corporate problems solved by your product

From your analysis, trends and patterns should emerge. If your analysis shows that most of your customers are mature, U.S.-based energy, utility or manufacturing companies with at least $1B in revenues, you're well on your way to defining the ICP and issuing marching orders to your marketing and sales teams. Although the ICP is normally based on an analysis of current customers, it can also be *aspirational*, i.e., the kind of companies your organization wants to target and sell to. Companies shifting their strategy or pursuing growth and new markets will find the aspirational ICP particularly useful.

When you're finished, your spreadsheet should look like the grid below:

ICP Criteria	Target #1	Target #2	Target #3
Industry	Energy	Utilities	Manufacturing
Revenue	$1B+	$5B+	$2B+
Buyers	VP IT, CIO	CRO, CIO	CEO, CIO
Geography	U.S.	U.S.	Global
Lifecycle	Mature	Growth	Declining

Another important application of the ICP is to help your company decide when to say "No." I come from the startup world, where cash is king and the sales organization pursues every inbound prospect, no matter how dubious. It's all about survival when you're a startup, and we don't have the luxury of turning away potential customers. On the other hand, straying from your ICP guidelines leads to disappointing results and wasted energy. **You may make the sale today, but the customer's long-term**

prospects are bleak because they don't fit the ICP. Eventually, they'll stop seeing value. Sadly, in most cases, the customer ends up canceling their contract as soon as it's up for renewal.

The immediate sting of telling unqualified prospects "No" is far less acute than losing forecasted deals or watching customers fail with your solution. The pressure to generate short-term revenue never subsides, but growth companies would be wise to define their ICP early and adhere to its guidelines.

* SHOWTIME *

With a clearly defined ICP, the salesforce can spot-check deals currently in the pipeline, initiate targeted prospecting efforts, and work with marketing to develop more effective outreach campaigns. Marketing has grown much more sophisticated in their use of advanced analytics to identify target markets and formulate a go-to-market approach, and this works to your advantage as you consider who to target and how to communicate your value proposition.

Increasingly, sales organizations are building the ICP criteria right into their CRM system, prompting reps to submit this information when they create a new opportunity. If a prospect meets 75% or more of the ICP criteria, then Sales should be bullish about the deal. Prospects meeting 50% or less of the ICP (like the white-hot prospect) need to be further qualified and forecast with caution. For the sales manager and CFO, applying the ICP filter brings a dose of realism to their sales projections and helps to adjust revenue expectations. While reps are using the ICP to target prospects, management uses the ICP to create a more realistic forecast and ensure that salespeople are focused on clients most likely to buy.

Build a strong relationship with your marketing team, because they can make or break your sales effort. As both teams begin to work from the ICP, marketing can be leveraged to initiate and run new outreach campaigns, build targeted lists, create case studies, run webinars, and determine the best events to attend.

Push your Marketing team to produce customer-success stories, because these will resonate with companies solving similar problems and trying to understand the ROI that they can expect from your solution.

A well-executed ICP strategy is key for companies trying to establish themselves as market leaders in their space. When you know exactly which prospects to target, you'll start to win with the top players, and this in turn will attract the smaller players. Before you know it, you're recognized as the premier solution and well on your way to building market dominance.

The deep expertise you develop through working with similar companies in your market enables you to claim the mantel of thought leadership, and for motivated salespeople, **it's an opportunity to climb aboard this train and build your own brand and reputation as a thought leader.** Believe me, your ideal customers are out there, and when you know exactly who they are, you're in a perfect position to sell to them.

#9: Go Social

Salespeople need to be proficient with social media because it's where their buyers connect, work, talk, and relax. You can conquer this brave new world with a smart and savvy social-selling strategy.

Consider the following statistics from a recent survey by the company Social Centered Selling:[5]

- 54% of salespeople have closed business as a direct result of using social media in the past year.
- 78% of salespeople use social media as part of their sales process.
- 72% of salespeople who use social media as part of their sales process outperform their peers.
- 92% of buyers say that they merely "hit delete" when an email or call comes in from someone they don't recognize.

Social media has been described as the convergence of *information* and *communication*, and the lesson is clear: if people like the information you're providing, they'll open the door and let you in. Taking advantage of social media to accelerate your sales effort requires an intelligent, focused approach, and a commitment to build and nourish your network with new content. Your social-selling strategy begins with *you*, and creating the right virtual persona to represent your professional brand is your first step.

Your Virtual Persona

Your online presence is your face to the world. **The social media profiles you create on services such as LinkedIn, Twitter, Facebook, Google+, Instagram and others will be seen by more people that you could ever meet in person.** This fact arguably makes your virtual persona the most important component of your professional brand. To master this brave new world of social selling, you must first understand its rules and nuances, and one of

---

[5] "Social Media and Sales Quota" survey.

the most important rules is that **nobody wants to be sold to in the social media universe.** This may require you to change your strategy and approach, but you need to adapt because this is where your buyers are. They're going online to research you, connect with each other, and bypass the marketing message to get the real scoop on your company. **Your virtual persona will either attract or repel potential buyers, so it's important to get it right.**

Let's review four of the top social media services for professionals:

LinkedIn ("LI")

LinkedIn is a business-oriented social networking site that enables users to post an online profile, find and connect with people they know and work with, post articles, participate in group discussions, exchange messages and more. LI is estimated to have **more than 433 million registered users.**

Twitter

Twitter is a social networking site that enables users to post condensed 140-character messages ("Tweets") to both the people in their network ("followers") and the wider universe of **310 million active Twitter users.**

Facebook

The largest of the social networking sites with **1.6 billion active users**, Facebook allows users to connect with "friends", post messages and pictures, receive notifications when their friends share content, and join common-interest groups.

Instagram

Instagram is a photo-and-video-sharing social networking site with **500 million active users**. Content on Instagram can be shared easily across a wide range of other social media sites, including Facebook, which acquired Instagram in 2012.

It can be overwhelming to keep track of the niche social sites that seem to spring up almost weekly, so for our purposes I'm going to recommend that you focus on **LinkedIn** and **Twitter** to start. I know salespeople who swear by Facebook, Instagram and Pinterest (among others), but I'd recommend investigating these services *only after* you've mastered social selling through LI and Twitter.

Once you've perfected your virtual persona and started building your network, it's imperative that you feed your audience with fresh content. An effective social-media strategy requires spending at least 15 to 20 minutes every day sharing articles, writing original content, contributing to discussion boards, and expanding your network.

There are five distinct advantages to going social, and each is important to developing your overall social-selling strategy:

1. Online Calling Card
2. Networking Tool
3. Communication Channel
4. Broadcast Platform
5. Resource for Research

Your Online Calling Card

Today, most prospective clients will get to know you **virtually** before they ever meet you in person. Your LI profile becomes your face to the world, detailing your expertise, work history, education, interests, publications, group membership and network of contacts. Twitter is a virtual library of your opinions, articles, perspectives, and videos. Collectively, they become your virtual brand that will attract potential clients and shape their perceptions of you and your company.

As a professional, you need to put forth a professional image. Spend the time required to create and maintain a compelling profile. You should always post a picture, and make sure it's studio-quality; visual images are powerful, so avoid using avatars, kitschy snapshots and caricatures. Your *Professional Summary* on LI and headline on Twitter are what people see first, so initial impressions matter. You need to create a powerful marquee for your brand that draws people in and lets them know about you.

I'm constantly tweaking my social media profiles, rewriting and updating them until I'm satisfied that they're current and present the right image. If you need ideas, browse through similar profiles and borrow ideas to improve your own profile. Expect that prospects, customers, competitors, colleagues and prospective employers will see your online calling card before they *ever* meet you in person, so commit to spending the necessary time to make your virtual presence the best it can be.

Powerful Networking Tool

I'm old enough to have actually owned a Rolodex, and I recall flipping through the wheel to find a business card when I needed to call a customer. Today your Rolodex is digital, and it's likely to include thousands of people in every country in the world. Social media has transcended borders and brought people together like never before, to the point where anyone with an Internet connection and a shared interest can become part of your extended network.

Your virtual persona is merely window dressing without a strong network. Once you're satisfied with your profile, your next task is to create an extensive network of business contacts. **LI has become so indispensible in my professional life that I include my LI address on my business card and email signature**. I'm constantly seeking to grow my network and keep people engaged by providing new and meaningful content. Whenever I meet a new contact, I make it a point to connect with that person on LI and Twitter. Every salesperson is looking for little clues to provide more insight into a customer's thought process, and social media can be quite useful in this regard.

The next time you're in the early stages of a promising sales cycle or engaged in a competitive bid, invite your new contacts to connect on LI. Whether they accept your invitation (or not) can speak volumes.

If they accept, it's reasonable to conclude that they see you as a potential partner. Most people don't litter their network with casual contacts. But if they decline, you may want to ask yourself why they don't want to connect with you. Not to make you paranoid, but your pending deal may be less promising than you think.

I'm very discerning with my LI network, much more so than with other social media services. I decline invitations from people I don't know. Likewise, I don't invite prospects to connect until I've had a conversation with them. When they know my name, they're more likely to accept my invitation. The opposite is also true.

Another advantage to building your network with care is LI *Connections*. It's based on the "six degrees of separation" concept, and essentially displays how many "acquaintance links" away you are from any other person on LI. It's very useful for referrals and introductions, and we know that these open doors more effectively than any cold call. If my network is full of people I don't really know, it's much harder to ask them for an introduction to someone I want to meet in their network. While expanding your LI network is key to your social strategy, exercise the proper degree of discretion. Remember, there's no prize for the salesperson with the most strangers in their network.

Unlike LI, Twitter values *quantity* of followers over *quality*, so your mission is to follow and be followed by as many people as you can. It's common for high-profile individuals and celebrities to have millions of Twitter followers. When I first joined Twitter, I chose several hashtags that represented my areas of interest— #sales, #innovation, #leadership and my hometown of #Boston— to quickly find and connect with like-minded people. Twitter recommendations make it fast and easy to expand your universe of potential contacts, and over time the size and diversity of your Twitter network will grow exponentially. You can set up an automatic response to new followers directing them to your website or related social media accounts, and in this way you ensure every component is contributing to the overall strategy.

Communication Channel

Many professionals—including your buyers—are more approachable and accessible through social channels than through phone and email. I've found that busy executives who never take my call *will* respond to a direct message on Twitter. A huge advantage of social messaging is that the usual filters don't exist: there's no EA screening your call, or spam filter routing your emails from the inbox to the trash. Because most people maintain their own social-media accounts, they'll receive your message *directly*. You'll have less competition as well; while executives may receive dozens of calls and emails from vendors every day, they'll only get one InMail or direct message (yours) on Twitter. If you're persistent without becoming a stalker, this kind of exclusivity gets you noticed.

Direct messages on LI are sent through InMail, a feature I use extensively to communicate with new prospects. Unlike Twitter, you can send *anyone* an InMail message, so InMail can be used to target both warm and cold prospects. I use InMail to send introductory messages to targeted people before I invite them to connect, and I also use it to set up meetings with CEOs and other executives when I know we'll be attending the same conference. The number of InMails you can send per month depends on your account level, and LI credits you for every sent InMail that doesn't generate a response.

Twitter enables you to post both public and private messages to other users. To send a public message, simply include the person's @username, and they'll be alerted to the fact that they were mentioned in a Tweet. The downside to this approach is that your message is in the public domain for everyone to see. Direct messaging is far preferable, delivering a private message to the recipient's Inbox. The catch is that this person already needs to be following you on Twitter to receive your direct message.

How do you compel a person to follow you on Twitter? You can ask them directly; you can mention them in a public post; you can "favorite" and retweet their postings to get their attention; and you can contact them through traditional means and ask them to follow you on Twitter. If they find your content relevant and interesting, chances are good that they'll become a follower. Unlike LI, Twitter followers are easy to amass, so it's not difficult to target certain individuals and work them into your network.

Broadcast Platform

Social media presents you with an unprecedented opportunity to broadcast messages to a very large audience. When you consider that new content is the lifeblood of the Internet, producing original articles and videos should be a cornerstone of your social-media strategy. Today's top sales professionals are not just salespeople, but thought leaders and subject-matter experts, who can teach customers something new about their business. Broadcasting your message through social media creates visibility for you and your brand, and builds trust with the audience. I'm often still surprised when people tell me that they've read my book or a recent article; it's a perfect icebreaker that usually leads to a positive conversation.

Social-media pros will have access to thousands of people through their direct networks on LI, Twitter, Facebook, Instagram, and others. The networking effect helps your message to ripple outwards, as people in your network share with others in their network, and so on. It's easy to see how your message could end up in front of hundreds of thousands of people in a single day. Every message that you broadcast—opinion pieces, blogs, articles, pictures and links—has the potential to spread like wildfire. Each post builds up your virtual persona, and over time you should aspire to become a leading resource for the topics you know and care about. That said, while positive content builds your persona, negative content can have exactly the opposite effect.

Always pause before you post, and ask yourself if this posting strengthens your brand, persona, and overall social media mission.

Be very aware that once your message is broadcast, it's beyond your control. Even if you delete it, it's still out there. There are a million stories about social-media mistakes, and you don't want to be one of them. Stick to a positive strategy, and resist the urge to be impulsive with postings.

Sharing content from others is great, but original content is what will set you apart. Sharpen your writing skills by starting a blog and then linking to it through your social media accounts. Set a goal of one new article (500 words) per month, and scale up your effort over time. One of the advantages of sales is that we're on the front lines constantly meeting new clients and encountering unique business situations. Your real-life experience gives you perspective and makes you stand out. **You're an expert in your industry, so let this expertise shine through in your articles and postings.** Plus, everyone knows that salespeople have the best stories, so use storytelling to convey your point and make your writing memorable.

While social media is an important part of your overall sales strategy, it's not a high-return investment. Think of it as a slow drip that will pay off over time. **Social media can be a huge drain on your time if you're not careful**, so I'd recommend no more than 20 minutes a day to start. This time can be split between LI and Twitter, and entails scanning the activity in your network; writing and commenting on posts; sharing articles; expanding your network; and participating in group discussions. Remember that while reposting an article is fine, creating your own original content is always better. Once you've developed a cadence, you'll see your network, reputation, and sphere of influence grow.

I strongly recommend getting to know the nuances of each social media service, and observe how advanced users work the system for maximum effect. For example, on Twitter #hashtags are your friend, and will help like-minded people find you. Choose three or four hashtags that best represent your interests and include these on every post. LI Groups offer discussion boards that attract people interested in specific topics, and LI *Pulse* is a collection of original blogs and articles visible to all members. You'll find that many of the prospects you want to reach are gathering at these destinations, and by participating you'll start having more conversations with the right people.

Research

While we all use the Web to research companies, social media provides unprecedented access to information about *people*. Smart salespeople use social media to find out what makes their prospects tick and to identify areas of common interest that can be used to open doors and develop rapport.

By scanning their social media profiles, you can find articles that your prospects have written, watch their speeches, view their comments on discussion boards, and even preview the conferences they'll be attending. If you're attending the same conference, send them InMail to arrange a meeting; I *guarantee* that your competitors are missing this trick. When you know something about a person, you can personalize your email or phone message to make sure it resonates and gets their attention. This is the *only way* to prospect in the digital age.

In the old days, salespeople would scan a prospect's office for pictures, awards and other clues about their interests. Today, LI provides a detailed picture of their work history, education, personal interests, networks, and publications. Twitter showcases their opinions and passions through links to content and personal opinions. Facebook provides a glimpse into their personal life: whether they're married with kids; their favorite sports team; what causes they support; and where they go on vacation. When you know more about the person across the table, you're better equipped to get their attention and start building rapport. Here are several bedrock rules of social media to keep in mind as you begin to **Go Social**:

It's about standing out

Everyone today has multiple social media accounts, including LI and Twitter. You need to differentiate yourself and stand out from the crowd. This requires discipline, planning and commitment. Make social media a part of your daily schedule and work on creating original content. **With a million stars in the sky, people are looking for the brightest lights; you need to be one of them.**

Perfect your virtual persona

Anyone visiting my LI account sees a professional picture and a marquee that advertises Jonathan Jewett. I worked my headline and summary for weeks until it was just right, and I still tweak it regularly. Take the time to create and maintain the virtual persona you want the world to see.

Don't mix business and pleasure

LI and Twitter are my business accounts, while Facebook is reserved for friends and family. I don't mix business and pleasure, and recommend that you do the same. Nobody wants business contacts viewing their goofy college photos.

Pause before you post

Did you publish personal pictures to your business site, get political or post a Tweet that you now regret? Treat every social media post as if it's permanent (because it is), and take a moment to reflect on it before you hit the *Post* button. Once you do, it's out of your control.

#10: Get LinkedIn

LinkedIn is arguably the most important business-networking tool available to professionals today. Optimize your LinkedIn strategy to strengthen your brand and start conversations with more of the right people.

Let's look at some LI statistics: [6]

Number of LI users (as of 2/4/16): 433 million users

Number of LI users in the United States: 107 million

LI's reach of the total U.S. digital population: 37%

Number of new LI users per second: 2

Although I've covered LinkedIn in **#9: Go Social**, LI is important enough to merit its own chapter. I won't review the mechanics of LI, because every salesperson—not permanently residing in digital purgatory—has at least set up a LI profile and made some connections by now. In a nutshell, LI enables you to look up and connect virtually with any person in the world who also has an active LI account. This includes your colleagues, the CEOs of Fortune 500 companies, and even their summer interns.

A person's LI profile contains a wealth of information about them: their current job and title, work history, education, colleagues, network connections, skills, interests, professional recommendations, publications and more. You can search for people and companies to build prospecting lists. You can broadcast and share new content with your network. You can see if people in your network are connected to your prospects and ask for introductions. When people join your network, you have an open line of communication with them through direct messaging. In short, it's one of the most important prospecting, networking and

---

[6] *Source:* http://expandedramblings.com/index.php/by-the-numbers-a-few-important-linkedin-stats/#.VD7S8ocUpUg

communication tools that a modern salesperson can leverage to do his/her job even better.

There are five distinct advantages to getting LinkedIn, and each is important to developing your overall LI strategy:

1. Networking
2. Referrals
3. Direct Messaging (InMail)
4. Brand-building
5. Sales Navigator

Networking

A strong network is indispensible to your success with LI. As you build your digital Rolodex of co-workers, clients, associates, friends and colleagues, you can correspond, keep in touch, track their careers, ask for recommendations and referrals, and share information. There are no limits on your ability to message people in your network, and this is one more incentive to build networks with qualified connections. Here are some best practices for LI networking:

- When you begin a new sales cycle with a prospect, send a LI connection request to your contacts. As we discussed in **#9: Go Social**, whether they accept your invitation or not can speak volumes about their intentions.
- As we'll explore later, some sales reps send a LI connection request to every inbound lead. Although there are pros and cons to this approach, it can generate a response when the normal cadence of emails and phone calls isn't working.
- If you meet a potential client and have any discussion of substance, send them an LI connection request. This works especially well for prospects you meet at trade shows, conferences, and networking events.
- Everyone receives random connection requests from people they don't know, so use your discretion when considering requests from unknown individuals. There's little benefit to building a network filled with people you don't know.

- Include your LI contact info on your business cards and email signature, and actively encourage people to connect with you.
- Optimize your profile with the right keywords so potential buyers, hiring managers, and search engines can find you.

Remember that a huge volume of LI connections is less important than the relationships you build with the people in your network. Deliver a personal touch by contacting people often, sending them articles, and recommending their posts. It doesn't do you any good to plant a huge field of sunflowers if you don't water them regularly, so keep this in mind as you execute on your networking strategy.

Referrals

One advantage of building a large and qualified network is your ability to ask for referrals to new prospects. LI is a viral service, meaning that once someone is part of your network, you can see everyone in *their* network as well. When you view a prospect on LI, you can see if you're connected to them through your extended network. When you find a mutual acquaintance, ask for an introduction. Warm referrals beat cold calls any day, so take full advantage of your network to begin conversations and open doors with new contacts

While I was helping a startup to build their sales program, every one of our initial clients was found through LI referrals. The CEO was amazed by how quickly I was able to fill up my pipeline with qualified prospects, and my results were head-and-shoulders above my peers. **Here's my secret**: I created a list of 20 target companies to start, and looked up all of them on LI. When you're viewing a company on LI, it displays a sidebar "How You're Connected," which shows all of your first- and second-degree connections. First-degree meant that I knew someone working at the target company, so I'd call this person and ask for an introduction to their head of Marketing. Taking a page from **#14: Your Customer's Little Black Book**, I'd also ask if they knew *anyone else* who might be interested in my product.

This strategy accomplished two things: (1) it gave me an internal referral at my target companies; and (2) it generated warm referrals at other companies that I then added to my target list. If I couldn't generate an internal or external reference at a particular company, I dropped it from the list and replaced it with a more promising target. **In this way, I was able to build a pipeline of twenty prospective clients without making a *single* cold call.** My entire pipeline of opportunities was built through RI referrals, and I was signing new customers while my colleagues were stuck making cold calls.

Direct messaging through InMail

InMail is LI's internal messaging platform that enables you to send unlimited messages to people within your network. LI does limit the number of InMails that can be sent to people *outside* of your network, but paid plans will give you more InMail credits for prospecting. The best way to gain access to people is to invite them into your network. Once they accept, InMail becomes yet another communication channel through which you can carry on a conversation. The initial challenge is encouraging new prospects to connect with you.

Let's assume that you've identified an individual who is a perfect candidate to buy your product, but neither of you know each other. You could send them a cold LI connection request, but they're likely to decline it. A better approach is to introduce yourself first through a phone call, email, or InMail message. Then, when you follow up with an LI connection request, they'll know who you are and why you want to connect. If they accept your invitation, you can assume it's because they're interested in talking. In this way, you qualify each other before a connection is made.

Some of my inside sales colleagues send a LI connection request to every single person who shows up as an inbound lead. I have mixed feelings about this approach, because while accepting your request can indicate interest, prospects come and go. I'd prefer not to have my LI network filled with random people I barely know, but this is a personal decision.

If you do choose to follow this strategy, here's a 6-touch cadence developed by my inside sales colleagues that they employ to pursue inbound leads over a 2-week period:

- Day 1: Introductory Email
- Day 4: Call
- Day 7: InMail
- Day 9: LI connection request
- Day 12: Call
- Day 15: Email

I like this approach because it's not completely cold; you've contacted the prospect several times before inviting them to connect. If you're unable to generate a response from a prospect with this cadence, it's probably a safe bet to assume that they're not interested and you can move on.

Building Your Brand

More people will see your LI profile than you could ever hope to meet in person. In many ways, it's your public face to the world, and often the first place a prospect will go to learn more about you. At its core, branding is all about perception; your task is to shape the way you *want* people to see you. While many people build their LI brand around their current role, I recommend taking a wider view and using LI to advertise your entire *career:* sales professional, executive, author, speaker, as well as current role/title. **You want LI to showcase the depth and breadth of your experience, because this is what a potential client gets when they work with you.**

Here are several tips to help you build your brand on LI:

- Make sure your profile is professional and reflects the image you want to convey. Browse through other sales profiles and steal good ideas.
- Write your own articles and post them to LI *Pulse.* Harness the full power of social media by cross-promoting your posts across all networks. Remember, thought leaders take

positions and offer opinions, so don't be afraid to take a stand and argue your position.

- Join groups of like-minded individuals and start group discussions around topics that interest you and showcase your expertise. Become a frequent contributor to these group discussions.
- Find and share one article about your industry every morning, then monitor the post's activity and respond to comments.
- If you're attending or, even better, *speaking* at a conference, always share this information on LI. It's a great way to set up meetings before you arrive.

Sales Navigator

For salespeople, Sales Navigator ("SN") is like LI on steroids. Although it's a paid service, many sales organizations will subsidize SN since they find it to be an incredibly useful tool for salespeople. The main advantage of SN is that it gives you a customized dashboard through which you can view and run all of your sales-related activities. Functionality like LeadBuilder helps you to create targeted prospecting lists of LI contacts based on highly-specific criteria. You can save prospects as "leads" in the system, meaning that you'll receive an update when they post a new article, participate in a discussion, or switch jobs. With this information, you can create personalized messages that will get their attention. SN also gives you additional InMail credits, allowing you to send even more prospecting messages to people outside of your network.

SN essentially takes all the sales-specific functions of LI and consolidates these in one place. It'll help you to be much more productive on LI and it's easy to use, so ask your manager to cover this expense. It won't be long before you're generating results and maximizing LI's potential to improve your overall sales performance.

#11: The Art of the RFP

Although they're a ton of work, RFPs very often result in sales. By actively seeking out RFPs and building a quick-response effort, you can ensure that this effort pays off.

Recently, a colleague and I were discussing one of our more successful competitors and looking for good ideas that we could steal and use to our advantage. When the subject of Requests for Proposal ("RFPs") arose, she revealed an interesting tidbit: our competitor had instituted a coordinated, outbound-calling effort targeting Procurement departments in the top 150 prospects in our marketplace. They were actively approaching Procurement with the following questions:

- Were there any active RFPs at the moment?
- Was their company expecting to issue any RFPs in the next six months?
- Could they send an information packet about their company and be contacted if/when any RFPs were issued?

As we contemplated our own lack of inbound RFPs for the past six months, I had a Eureka moment: **the overall demand hadn't slowed down; instead, our competitor had cornered the market and left us out in the cold!** While we'd been waiting for the buyers to come to us, our competitors had been actively courting them and, in some cases, taking an active role in writing the RFP. The next day, we brought a plan to our CEO to aggressively pursue RFPs in our market, and over time we saw this strategy pay off and even become a competitive advantage. As we won more RFP bids, our sales and revenue numbers saw a similar uptick.

As discussed in **#1: Rewrite the Rulebook**, the sales rep who gets to a prospect first is in an excellent position to influence their thinking and shape their requirements. The same principle applies to this technique, as every sales organization will seize the opportunity to write a prospect's RFP. Love 'em or hate 'em, the irrefutable fact is that RFPs usually result in a sale for *someone*, and your job is to make sure it's *you*.

The best-case scenario for RFPs is that the prospect lets you help them create their RFP document. These are the types of deals you *know* you'll win. Your next best option is to learn about a pending RFP while there's still time to connect with and influence the business unit. If you're calling around to find pending RFPs, chances are you'll find them. When you do, Sales should be on the phone immediately to the business unit. Finally, there are "blind RFPs" that show up without warning. Assuming your competitor didn't write the RFP, your ability to win blind RFPs depends on developing a finely-tuned process that leverages your best people and a searchable library of past RFP responses that can be used to populate a new response. Whether you're maneuvering for the inside track or developing a rapid-response capability, mastering the art of the RFP is a core competency for any sales organization that will lead directly to more closed deals and increased revenue.

* GAME PREP *

You need to identify any active prospects that are leaning toward issuing an RFP. When you find them, first ask if they'll just buy from you and forget about issuing the RFP altogether. (Strangely enough, this *does* happen!) But if they're committed to the RFP process, take a page from **#1: Rewrite the Rulebook** and offer your Requirements List to help them define their requirements. When a prospect adopts your requirements as their own, you have a built-in advantage to win the RFP bid and the ensuing business. **Remember, the best way to win the RFP is to help the prospect write the RFP.** The minute a prospect mentions the possibility of an RFP, do your best to talk then out of it. If this doesn't work, make sure you're an active partner and influencer in the RFP creation process.

Of course you won't be in active discussions with every company contemplating an RFP, and this is why you need an outbound calling effort targeting Procurement departments. Although it could be argued that searching for future RFPs is a higher-value activity than cold-calling, I wouldn't advocate that salespeople run this campaign themselves. Your time is better spent working with clients and closing deals. A far better scenario is to leverage inside sales to make these calls with the goal of identifying any active or pending RFPs and request that your company be invited to participate. When potential RFPs are identified, the sales team is notified and can take a more active role engaging the client.

When speaking with Procurement, you want to broadly define your product offerings and value proposition. For example, if you sell software that enables secure online transactions, ask to be included in any RFPs dealing with security, finance and transaction processing. You can always decline to respond to an RFP that isn't a good fit, but **your goal is to make the vendor shortlist with as many prospects as possible**. Don't limit yourself from the outset by defining your solution in narrow terms.

As your team calls, you're certain to come across RFPs already in process. **Never** let them tell you it's too late for you, and **always** pull out the stops to get your company included. Beg, plead, and charm the Procurement contact if you have to, and emphasize that they *owe it to their organization to include a market leader like you in their evaluation*. You can only win if you're invited to participate, so do whatever you can to make this list.

When you come across pending RFPs, meaning that they will be issued at a future date, capture all the specifics, including dates, scope, business sponsors, and budget. Request that your name be added to the vendor shortlist, and email all relevant information about your company to the Procurement contact immediately. Circle the RFP issue date on your calendar, and call Procurement the week before to double-check that you've been included.

The beauty of future RFPs is that you have time to contact the business unit to influence their thinking and—with a little luck—help them write the RFP. This is a big advantage; once RFPs have been issued and are active, many procurement groups will demand you deal only with them and prohibit you from communicating with the businesspeople. *There are no such limitations for future RFPs*. Most vendors don't have an outbound program focused on finding RFPs, and this means there's a good chance that you'll be there first. If you're serious about winning at the RFP game, you need to make RFP solicitations an active part of your outbound calling effort.

* SHOWTIME *

Sales organizations have different approaches when it comes to responding to RFPs, from rapid-response teams that specialize in RFPs to simply handing the document to a salesperson and asking them to handle it. Regardless of your approach, the first step is to review the document thoroughly from start to finish. I'd recommend the salesperson and at least one product expert complete this review, and you'll need to answer the following high-level questions:

- How well does our product fit the stated requirements?
- What's the magnitude of effort to respond by the due date?
- Do we see any terms/concepts indicating that one of our competitors wrote the RFP?
- Can we win?

These questions will drive your decision as to whether your company will respond or not. **Only respond to RFPs that you strongly believe you can win.** If you've written the RFP, you *know* you can win. For all others, your success is wholly dependent upon the strength of your written response. While we always want to produce a masterpiece, the reality is that competing priorities often make it difficult to spend quality time on RFPs. Given these constraints, **your best bet is to maintain a database of past RFP responses that can be quickly copied and pasted to complete as much of the current RFP as possible.**

This strategy works because customer requirements usually don't vary significantly; the majority are looking for the same basic business functions and value. It's likely that your stock answers can be used again and again for RFP responses. Once finished, review every question and ensure that your stock answers are actually addressing the buyer's intent. Buyers want a custom response; not a collection of pasted answers that don't provide the data they need. For quality purposes, every RFP should by thoroughly reviewed by at least two people before it's submitted back to the prospect. Here are some tried-and-true best practices to help your company truly master *The Art of the RFP*:

my demand, I convened my sales team and we decided to take control of our own destiny.

Every salesperson was assigned one blog post per week. Others volunteered to write articles, and my sales engineer committed to finishing a white paper he had begun. Without any help from Marketing, our small sales team had developed its own content strategy, and our mandate was simple: *demonstrate to potential buyers that we understand the problems they're trying to solve.* Since I like to write, it was more fun than work, and over time some very interesting things began to happen.

The first was that I was quickly perceived to be much more credible; customers would engage me in conversation and mention specific points from my articles and blog posts. Second, I saw a wave of *new* followers on Twitter and LI that expanded my reach exponentially. Third, my pipeline grew as my phone began ringing, and I started having more conversations with qualified prospects. The constant drumbeat of communication was generating results and prompting people to take action.

My sales team saw similar results, and we realized that we were actually becoming thought leaders in our space. Even though we initially viewed ourselves as [just] salespeople, the reality was that **our daily experience put us on the front lines of the business, and this gave us unique perspective on the challenges that companies faced.** We were as qualified as anyone to offer our observations and opinions, and people loved our articles. It wasn't hard to develop a voice; the hard part was finding the time and discipline to write an article or record a video. Once we committed to producing this content on a regular basis, we overcame the biggest obstacle to creating a more effective content strategy.

* GAME PREP *

Your content strategy depends on a producing a steady stream of content and then distributing it to a target audience. Here's a list of possible media to get you started:

most prevalent and most appropriate for building your virtual salesforce.

Appointment-Setters (outsourced)

These are high-volume callers with a mandate to schedule introductory calls with prospects on your behalf. Prospect qualification is often light, so it's important to provide these callers with a good list of companies and titles that meet your ICP. You can expect an average of 10-15 new appointments per caller per month. As the focus is on *quantity* of appointments over *quality*, this is a good resource if your goal is simply to talk to as many prospects as possible.

- *Cost:* Ranges from $500 to $800 per lead by professional callers, but many companies hire temps or college kids for less.
- *Pros:* Inexpensive; can generate many prospects in a short timeframe; minimal training and support required.
- *Cons:* Prospects aren't deeply qualified; callers may be unable to handle in-depth questions or objections; callers are less experienced, so not a good option if you're targeting executives.

Sales Development (outsourced)

As of this writing, Sales Development ("SD") is the hot new trend in business. Recognizing that field salespeople are prohibitively expensive cold-callers, SD's mandate is to contact and qualify a prospect before they're passed to senior salespeople to begin working their magic. There are dedicated SD providers as well as independent agents who can help you in this pursuit.

Outsourced SD can be counted on to qualify deals and prospects before sales even sees them, thus ensuring that the sales organization is working on the deals most likely to close. Outsourced SD costs more and requires more training than appointment-setters, so ask your manager about your sales organization's willingness to fund this effort.

- *Cost:* Ranges from $3K to $10K per month depending on the number of callers, seniority and how far they're expected to drive the sales cycle.
- *Pros:* Callers are more senior and can run a more complete sales cycle; customer experience is more seamless since callers can represent themselves as part of your extended team.
- *Cons:* Can be expensive as volume increases.

Sales Development (in-house)

Hiring or recruiting full-time people to call on your behalf is a favored approach among large sales organizations. Many organizations will pair these resources with counterparts in field sales, and this gives you the ability to direct their activities. The function of inside reps ranges from appointment setting to carrying a quota and closing deals. At Oracle, for example, the field rep owned a total quota for the territory, and the inside rep contributed to this by closing transactional deals and prospecting for the overall territory. If you have access to in-house SD, I recommend that you take every opportunity to leverage this resource to your advantage.

- *Cost:* These people are full-time employees and receive a salary from your company, so they won't cost you anything.
- *Pros:* Trained by your organization; usually more experienced and professional; most can run a sales cycle; intimate knowledge of your products and pitch.
- *Cons:* They may not report directly to you or be shared resources, decreasing your ability to direct their activities.

* GAME PREP *

Your budget and resource availability are your first considerations when building a virtual salesforce. A budget of zero precludes you from making progress on this front, and a self-funded campaign can also limit your options. That said, I'd contend that *any* additional sales resource working on your behalf is a huge plus. There may even be budget available to you; I currently give each of my reps $5K a year to spend any way they choose. Some of the use it, some of them don't, and many don't even know it's available. You won't know unless you ask, so **ask your manager for a budget to build your virtual team**. When you secure your funding, I can guarantee a stampede behind you as your colleagues follow your lead.

Your virtual salespeople don't always need to be new hires; assess what resources already exist in your company and how you can take advantage of these. Even if you can't secure a person to help you full-time, ask for a resource for three months of outbound calling. This activity blitz will make a big impact on your pipeline. It can only help your case if you've developed a solid plan around how you'll use these resources, so clearly define their activities and expected return. Managers will be more inclined to work with you if they see that you're organized and will put this person's time to good use.

If you're hiring outside resources, a Google search can connect you with many firms specializing in appointment-setting and outsourced SD. Posting an inquiry to sales groups on LinkedIn will yield both recommendations and solicitations, so be prepared for lots of sales inquiries. Think about what it is that you're looking for in a partner, and use the questions below to qualify your candidates:

- What's your specialty or area of focus?
- How far can I expect you to progress the sales cycle?
- What channels do you use to contact prospects (phone/email/social media)?
- What's the time and resource commitment I can expect from your firm?
- What support and materials do you need from me?
- How do people get trained?
- Who supplies the call lists?
- Will you represent yourself as an employee of my company? If so, how do we ensure a seamless customer experience?
- Will you require a company email address and access to internal calendars for scheduling?

- How do you charge? What's the commitment period? What's considered a "bad lead" and do I pay for these?
- May I speak with two of your clients as references?

You should expect to supply call scripts, email templates, collateral, an ICP profile, and training resources. Some firms maintain their own database of companies and people to call, while others will ask you to furnish them with a specific list. For firms paid to generate a high volume of leads, they may ask you for five thousand names (or more) to get started. If you're supplying lists, make sure they're current and accurate; you don't want callers wasting billable time looking up phone numbers. Your best bet is to mine your database to produce a list, so always look internally before buying a list from an external vendor.

Your virtual salesforce is an excellent laboratory for experimentation. You can use them to test new messaging, targets, contacts, markets, and promotions. As the team becomes more proficient with your value proposition and pitch, they'll adapt to these small changes without losing their effectiveness. Big changes, however, may require additional training and resources before the virtual team can act, so be prepared and provide what's needed.

While calling companies on the phone is a big part of the prospecting effort, in the digital age most firms have extended their outreach to include email, social media and even content syndication. It's all about attracting the prospect's attention, and many people will respond to email or social media messaging before they'll answer a cold call. *When working with an outside firm, their approach should mirror your own.* If your sales efforts incorporate social media and content syndication, your virtual salesforce should extend and supplement these efforts. It's important for prospects to see you as a cohesive team, so do your best to minimize confusion and ensure a unified approach and seamless customer experience.

* SHOWTIME *

Once your virtual salesforce begins to crank up its efforts, it's your job to motivate and train them, provide target lists and call scripts, set goals, monitor their progress, and hold them accountable for results. New appointments will start showing up quickly, so prepare yourself for this influx and make sure you're ready to run with these new leads.

The lead-handoff process is important to get right, because mistakes are highly visible and can potentially confuse prospects. Clearly define the point at which a qualified lead should be transitioned from the callers to you, and monitor this process closely. A dropped lead can mean a missed opportunity, so make sure the handoff process is tight. Many outside firms will represent themselves as employees of your firm, and they'll need company emails and access to systems like the calendar and CRM if they're expected to work like any other member of your team.

You're the boss, so manage the virtual salesforce as if they were direct reports. Set targets and measure progress against goals. Schedule regular checkpoint calls to discuss progress and challenges. Every lead needs to be documented in your CRM, and meet the agreed-upon "lead" criteria before you pay for it. If efforts are exceeding expectations, raise the bar and push the team even harder. If they're falling short, identify the problems and fix them. You can either set your virtual team up to succeed or fail, so be sure to help them and take an active interest in their progress.

"Chief Motivator" is one more hat for you to wear, because it's often up to you to rally the troops and keep them focused on goals. Prospecting and cold-calling are tough; even seasoned callers get discouraged when everyone seems to be telling them "No." For this reason, it's important to celebrate the small victories. A little friendly competition always works, and contests and incentives can keep people motivated when the going gets tough.

The best outsourcing firms get to know your product well, internalize your pitch, and become familiar with the market. They can become self-sufficient very quickly. When you check references, ask if your potential partner takes this kind of initiative. Managing a virtual salesforce can consume your time when they're struggling, but it's a completely different experience when they're performing well and keeping your calendar filled with new calls and appointments.

A quick note for managers on structuring the sales team: I can't tell you how many times I've seen companies hire expensive salespeople before they've built the demand infrastructure to support them. This leads to senior people being forced to make cold calls to fill their pipeline, which is a terrible use of resources. Instead, hire one senior salesperson to close the deals, and invest in building the sales machine to support them. When the senior rep has more leads than he/she can handle, hire another senior rep to balance the workload. In this way, you can keep costs aligned with revenue, provide scalability, and keep your people productive and happy.

#14: Open Your Customer's Little Black Book

Every referral or introduction a client makes on your behalf can be sales gold. Ask your clients to open their little black books and introduce you to their friends and colleagues. You'll boost your pipeline immediately and have even more conversations with receptive prospects.

Some of the fastest deals I've ever closed originated from customers who introduced me to people they knew who then also became my clients. **Open Your Customer's Little Black Book** starts with the simple act of asking current customers for two or three introductions to people they believe could use and benefit from your products.

There's a reason why senior salespeople rely on networking and referrals almost exclusively to build their pipeline: it works. When a trusted individual opens the door for you, you achieve instant credibility that otherwise could take months to build. Your customer is vouching for you as a potential business partner. They're willing to lift the velvet rope and let you into their world. Their referral will help you to immediately capture the prospect's attention, and you'll move to the front of the queue. With your bona fides established, you can skip ahead in the sales cycle and push deals to closure with greater velocity.

The importance of referrals has only been enhanced in this age of hyper-distraction. With the advent of social media, cell phones and wearable devices, vendors can reach you anywhere, anytime, through any device. We're constantly bombarded *en masse* with solicitations from unknown sources, all demanding our immediate attention. As a result, we've developed defense mechanisms that shut out extraneous noise to keep us focused. Two of these are what I refer to as the *Inbox* and the *Trashcan*.

The Inbox contains messages that capture our attention and are worthy of our time. Personally, I'd estimate that 1 in 20 communications actually reach my Inbox. Everything else gets sent to the Trashcan, including unsolicited junk and generic sales pitches that fail to capture my interest. Needless to say, the Trashcan is usually overflowing at the end of each day. For most of us, it takes about three seconds to decide whether a message belongs in the Inbox or the Trashcan. Ninety-five percent of unsolicited communications end up in the Trashcan, and this is why I instruct my sales reps to stop sending mass emails and cold-calling prospects: it just doesn't work anymore.

What *does* work every time is a personal call or note from a trusted source introducing you to someone they know. This message is guaranteed to make it into the recipient's Inbox, and gives you permission to start a sales cycle. **Your challenge is to make it into the Inbox of as many prospects as possible**. The reward is a bigger pipeline of qualified leads that can be quickly converted into solid sales opportunities.

Asking for referrals is the easy part; it's harder to hold your customers to this commitment without bothering them too much. Let's explore how to perform this balancing act with relative ease, initiate a referral request, and nurture your customer base to become an ongoing source of warm leads for you.

* GAME PREP *

First, think about which customers you feel comfortable asking for a referral. Start with your strongest relationships (customers who love you) as they are an assured "Yes." Long-time clients and those who are excelling with your solution can also be counted on to provide a reference. In terms of the right individuals to ask, approach people who are personally benefitting from your solution and senior people who are influential and highly networked. **People tend to introduce you to their peers, and senior-level contacts will introduce you to other senior-level contacts**. Since these people are often the decision-makers, executive referrals can accelerate your sales cycle and lead to faster results.

Today's average professional will work for seven different companies over their career, and this fact works to your advantage. A large and diverse network means that your customer can open many doors at many companies. This diversity enables you to be a bit more discerning, and specifically request contacts at companies meeting your ICP. When you ask for a referral, be clear about whom you'd like to be introduced to, and that you'll be following up with the express purpose of pitching your company. This is how I ask my customer's for a referral:

> *"Hal, you've been a good customer for a long time and I know you're seeing real value with my products. I was wondering if you might be willing to introduce me to two or three of your colleagues at other companies who you think might also benefit from my solution."*

It's natural to feel some apprehension when asking customers to recommend you, but it's actually a modest request. Put yourself in their shoes and imagine that a trusted vendor had approached you with the same question. You can probably think of a dozen friends, peers, colleagues, co-workers (past and present), partners and acquaintances who would be open to a conversation. I've made this request of many customers over the years, and I've never received a negative response. I believe this is because (1) I approach the right people, (2) I work hard to keep my customers happy, and (3) most professionals realize the power of networking and that it may be *them* asking *you* for a referral in the future. Every experienced networker knows that referrals are a two-way street, and they're prepared to give as much as they get.

So you've asked for a referral and the customer has agreed. **While their intentions may be good, execution is another story.** I've had customers enthusiastically volunteer to introduce me all over town, but a month later they hadn't lifted a finger on my behalf. There's no malice here; just busy people with their hearts in the right place and little free time. Be respectful, but also ask for relative timeframes when your customer agrees to make an introduction. "So you'll let me know next week when you connect with Sheila?" is a reasonable question, and it establishes your timetable for follow-up activities. Gentle reminders may be required along the way, and always remember that the customer is doing you a favor. When you've verified that contact has been made, it's your job to follow up and begin a conversation.

* SHOWTIME *

In addition to contacting the right people, the customer's endorsement is the most important element of this technique, and it will set the tone for your first call with the prospect.

The best-case scenario: Your customer calls their friend and gives you a glowing recommendation, sending you straight into their Inbox. When you connect, the prospect already feels like they know you and greets you warmly. I always ask conversation to make a call on my behalf because conversations are better than emails. If they send an email on your behalf, ask your customer to copy you on the message so you can see what was written and know when to schedule your follow-up.

A more common scenario: Your customer agrees to let you use their name, but it's up to you to reach out to the prospect. "Feel free to call Sheila Williams and use my name," they say. This makes your job harder—though not impossible—because you don't have an explicit recommendation coming directly from the customer. From your perspective, it's still a cold call. In this case, your best bet is to put your customer's name front and center in your messaging, and make it clear that you're calling because your shared acquaintance Hal Stanley asked you to call them.

With any referral, your goal is to make it into the prospect's Inbox and initiate a follow-up action. A verbal or written endorsement guarantees that you make it into their Inbox, while an OK to use someone's name is still a cold call and requires a bit more finesse. To make sure you're not relegated to the Trashcan, drop the name of your mutual contact right away in a voicemail or email:

> *"Hello Sheila, this is Jonathan Jewett. Hal Stanley gave me your name and recommended that I call you. Hal is a long-time customer of mine, and he thought you'd be very interested in learning more about my company. I was hoping we could find a time to talk."*

When sending email, the subject line should also showcase your customer's name: *Referral from Hal Stanley*. It's the customer's name—not yours—that will compel the prospect to pay attention, and Sheila may even call Hal to ask him about me before she responds. *Always* follow up on referrals because it's one of your best sources for new business, and it shows that you respect the gesture from your customer. Neglecting to follow up on a referral will ensure that your customer never does this favor for you again.

When you do the math, the potential impact of this technique becomes apparent. If you ask 10 customers for 3 referrals each, that's **30 high-value prospects in your deal pipeline**. When you compare this to the time and magnitude of effort to find 30 good prospects through cold-calling or email blasts, you can see why top salespeople rely on customer referrals exclusively to build their pipeline.

As with many of *The 40 Best*, this technique relies on a strong foundation of satisfied customers who will endorse both your company and you personally. It's a reality check of your customer's satisfaction with you, and their response will speak volumes because *nobody* is going to introduce a subpar vendor to people in their network. Customers who feel loved and see a strong ROI with your products, on the other hand, will be more than willing to share their success with friends and colleagues.

A last note on referrals: I like to make a gesture of gratitude whenever a customer helps me. It's a small thing that goes a long way. Handwritten thank-you cards are memorable and rare in the age of email and 140-character Tweets. If the introduction leads to a new deal, I might send along a gift basket or bottle of wine. If your company supports a referral program, customers might even receive product discounts or other incentives to make introductions on your behalf. Everyone appreciates gratitude, and a heartfelt "Thank You" or small gift will increase the likelihood that your customers open their little black book for you time and time again.

#15: Run a Webinar

Internet broadcasting empowers you to deliver a targeted message and Call-to-Action to a large audience at a low cost. Increasingly, companies are realizing the power of the webinar and making it a key component of their customer outreach strategy.

I'm a night owl who considers late-night product infomercials to be much more than just annoying distractions; they're also market research for sales professionals. Love 'em or hate 'em, you can't ignore them, and the numbers prove that infomercials work, driving millions of dollars in sales for products that most of us would never look at twice in the store. While most companies don't have the right products (or budget) for television advertising, B2B salespeople can learn from our B2C colleagues and harness the power of broadcasting to drive better results. Webinars are an inexpensive, easy and effective way to tell your story and mobilize the power of Web broadcasting to sell more products.

Web broadcasting tools like GoToWebinar empower you to create your own personal broadcast channel and run an unlimited number of webinars. You can invite a highly-targeted audience, control the message, hold an interactive discussion, and bring your message to life with the power of pictures, and video. Sales can produce their own branded infomercials that deliver a targeted pitch and a strong Call-to-Action. With a low price point and global reach, it's no surprise savvy companies have embraced webinars as a powerful channel to supercharge marketing and lead-generation efforts.

In many organizations, Marketing has responsibility for creating and running webinars. Sales departments need to recognize the power of webcasting and take control of this to achieve their own goals. Like the TV spot wizards of B2C selling know, products like the Garden Weasel and the Pocket Fisherman don't sell because they're great products; *they sell because they're presented in a compelling way that draws people in.* You need to make webinars part of your sales platform to connect with likely prospects, create a narrative, and present a Call-to-Action that results in a sale.

* GAME PREP *

Although webinars can be produced quickly and for minimal cost, they do require planning. Someone needs to craft the message and prepare the content. You may need to slot your webinar in between other webinars on the corporate calendar. IT needs to be on deck to operate the technical aspects while you're busy presenting. Working out these internal logistics is your first step. Once the production machine begins to hum, you need to choose a date. Give yourself plenty of time to prepare and potential attendees the notice they need to clear their calendars. Lunchtime webinars are often well-attended because the noon hour is natural downtime, and people can listen in while they eat. Once you've clarified the *how* and *when* of your webinar, you can work on developing the event itself. Preparation should focus on five areas: Tone, Topic, Content, Audience, and Call-to-Action.

The **Tone** sets the stage for your event. Unlike hard-selling TV infomercials, B2B sales are all about education and problem-solving, and the tone is softened accordingly. You can still promote a hard sell, but keep in mind that you're creating relationships on top of driving transactional sales. **The formula I recommend for a 1-hour webinar is to spend the first 45 minutes presenting your content and making your pitch, and the final 15 minutes on live Q&A.** Educate the attendees and then make your pitch, and experiment with different formats to see what works best with your target audience.

The **Topic** needs to be timely, relevant, and interesting to your audience. People simply won't attend if the topic doesn't resonate with them. For Sales teams focused on revenue, new product launches make for excellent webinars. I ran one webinar that provided a sneak-peek at a brand-new product, and concluded with a strong Call-to-Action offering a significant discount to anyone who bought within 30 days. I recorded the first sale of the new product, and subsequently made many more. Customer stories, testimonials, and discussions of key industry trends and challenges also make for compelling webinar topics that will ensure good attendance.

Once the Topic is defined, you can develop your **Content**. Since it's a broadcast medium, you need to keep your audience engaged. Compelling visuals, storytelling, customer narratives, interactive Q&A and video will capture the audience's attention and hold it. While PowerPoint slides are reliable (albeit boring), videos, pictures and live product demonstrations create a more memorable experience. Production value is important, so spend what's required to make it professional; your first sale will more than cover your costs. As you produce and run more webinars, work with your marketing group to publish these for viewing on your website. A robust library of topical webinars is a great resource for sales to hook new prospects.

Unless the webinar is highly targeted, your **Audience** should be as big as possible. Blast everyone in your database with an invitation, assume that 1 in 20 will RSVP, and estimate that half of the RSVPs will actually attend. A webinar with 75 to 100 people is a well-attended event, and will give your salespeople plenty of leads to pursue post-event. Every attendee becomes a potential prospect, so make sure to capture the RSVP and attendance lists and then deliver these to your sales team *the next day* for follow-up.

Unless it's purely educational, every webinar should include a **Call-to-Action**. You've spent time and energy getting people hooked, and now it's time to reel them in. Whether you want them to buy now, fill out a form, or schedule a demonstration, ASK the attendees to take this next step with you. Don't feel as though you have to build up to a big pitch at the end, either; you'll miss attendees who had to drop off early. Instead, deliver a series of mini-pitches throughout your presentation and make a final pitch before the webinar concludes. Send a follow-up email to everyone that thanks them for attending, repeats your Call-to-Action, and provides a link to the webinar replay on your website. Meanwhile, your salespeople are hitting the phones to answer questions and stay top-of-mind with your potential buyers.

* SHOWTIME *

Running webinars is a team effort. To ensure a good experience for your audience, make sure that your internal team is clear on their roles and responsibilities. For example, the presenter should focus on delivering the message, while other team members are prioritizing questions from the audience or making technical adjustments. Be sure to have a platform expert on-hand for every webinar; you don't want any tech glitches distracting the presenter or disrupting their rhythm.

The good news is that webinar software is reliable and straightforward to use, and your skills will improve as you run more of them. Practice never hurts, and I'd strongly recommend an internal run-through before the live event. With each webinar, you're creating a new video for your webinar library and building your content collection. When the webinar concludes, post the replay to your website as soon as possible and let everyone know it's there for viewing.

There are many different formats that can work for a webinar, so experiment and choose those that generate the best results. Watch how other companies run their webinars and steal their good ideas. Some webinars involve a full hour of presentation. Others are more fluid, with a high degree of interactivity with the audience. One of my most successful webinars was an interview with three of my customers, all of whom joined using Skype and said nice things about my company. This webinar replay became one of our most popular because people *like* to see other companies endorsing your products.

Explore real-time polling to get a pulse on the sentiment of the audience, and find out what messages are resonating. Webinar technology enables you to take full advantage of video and multimedia, and this can create a memorable and exciting presentation. Your goal is to engage the audience and make sure they sign up for your next webinar, so work hard to provide the best experience possible.

If you're running live Q&A during your webinar, take as many questions as you can during the live event. For all unanswered questions, follow up with an email answer within 48 hours. Attendees will appreciate the gesture, and it demonstrates your commitment to your customers.

One final point: many companies schedule their webinars to run during lunchtime, and this is smart for two reasons. First, although people may hesitate to sit in on a webinar during working hours, they *will* attend while eating lunch at their desks. Second, many people keep their midday hours open, increasing the likelihood that they'll be able to attend. *It doesn't matter how good your webinar is if nobody shows up.* With smart planning, webinars will become an indispensible part of your sales effort, and help you build your brand, educate prospective clients, and sell more widgets.

PART THREE

Go for the Jugular

In 1964, two academics, David Mayer and Herbert Greenberg, published an article in the *Harvard Business Review* titled "What Makes a Good Salesman." Building on past research and their own field study with insurance agents, Mayer and Greenberg postulated that successful salespeople must possess at least two basic qualities to be successful: **empathy** and **ego drive**. They wrote:

> *The salesman's empathy, coupled with his intense ego drive, enables him to hone in on the target effectively and make the sale. He has the drive, the need to make the sale, and his empathy gives him the connecting tool with which to do it."*

While many of the other sections in this book focus on building relationships, **Go for the Jugular** is about unleashing your ego drive—often referred to in sales as the "killer instinct."

A finely-tuned killer instinct is often what separates the best from the rest in sales. The techniques in this section are power plays that get right to the point, whether it's asking for the business, engaging the executive, or presenting an unimaginably bold vision. When you combine killer instincts with proven techniques (like *The 40 Best*), you *will* dominate the leaderboard, occupy a permanent spot at President's Club, and make more money.

Over my career, I've grown to realize the value of assertiveness and how it can fundamentally shift the balance of power in the sales cycle. It's made a big difference in my career, and helped me to develop the *swagger* that every confident salesperson needs.

The 8 techniques presented in **Go for the Jugular** are:

#16: The Big Audacious Proposal
Always ask for more than you think you can get, because sometimes you *do* get it.

#17: Nail the Pilot

Today, every company wants to try before they buy. When you nail the pilot, you'll make the sale. This technique is all about running a flawless evaluation process that will set you up perfectly for the bigger deal.

#18: ASK for the Business

Never underestimate the power of the ASK. Asking for a client's business is one of the simplest and most powerful actions you can take. You'll accelerate your deals and knock down the obstacles standing between you and a signed contract.

#19: A Taste of Honey

You know that your products are irresistible. Give your prospects a little taste to get them hooked and you'll have a customer for life.

#20: Solve Their Big Hairy Problem

The Big Hairy Problem is what keeps your clients awake at night. Solve it for them and you'll be rewarded with bigger deals and revered as a strategic partner.

#21: Let's Make a Deal

Learn what your prospects value most, and then make them an offer they can't refuse.

#22: Plan to Close with a Close Plan

Once the customer says "Yes," the hard work really begins. By detailing every step in your process and by making both sides accountable for a signed contract, the Close Plan ensures that your deal gets done.

#23: Make an Executive Play

Your sales career depends on your ability to connect and work with executives and decision-makers. By engaging with the leaders who make things happen, you can maneuver around endless sales cycles and indecisive project teams.

#16: The Big Audacious Proposal

Always ask for more than you think you can get, because sometimes you do *get it.*

"Be bold and mighty forces will come to your aid."
- Johann Wolfgang van Goethe, German writer and statesman

It's been said (and I happen to agree) that people sell the same way that they buy. If you're a naturally cautious buyer who shops around for the best price before eventually making a decision, as a sales rep you'll assume that your prospects are also going to shop around before deciding. If you're a reckless buyer, you'll push your prospects to make a fast decision and get impatient when they don't. Whether you realize it or not, you're projecting your own beliefs and patterns onto your prospects, and this invariably becomes a major influence on your selling style.

The Big Audacious Proposal ("BAP") is all about becoming the "big-game hunter" in your organization who can create and close the blockbuster deals. Everyone wants to close the big deals, but we're limited more by our beliefs and attitudes about sales than the customer's potential willingness to make a significant investment. The reps at the top of the leaderboard have already figured this out and developed the *cojones* to put themselves on the line and push the customer for a bigger commitment. Why? Because they know a little secret: **always ask for more than you think you can get, because sometimes you** *do* **get it.** In other words, go big or go home. This is the essence of the BAP.

By definition, the BAP is a bold proposal that challenges both you and the customer to think and act BIG. In your mind, you have absolutely no business proposing it in the first place, but by expanding your thinking and ambitions you've taken the first step towards becoming a sales big-game hunter. BAPs need to be visionary, exciting, and backed up by a compelling ROI and business case to work. Sign one or two of these deals and you've made your year; close them consistently and they'll define your career.

It all begins with you, and whether you can overcome the limits you place on yourself. As "The Great One" Wayne Gretzky once said, "**you miss 100 percent of the shots you never take**."

Below are two examples of BAP success and one example of failure, all of which hold important lessons. First, the BAP that worked: I was engaged by a department head to equip his small team with an instance of my software platform. The safe bet was to take down the small transaction and celebrate the win, but I believed there was more potential. Stepping back to take a fresh look at the environment, I saw a definite need in *two other* divisions for my product immediately, and the possibility of adding *three more* divisions within a year. Although five divisions could benefit from my product, the companywide need was undiscovered.

I asked my contact to set up a meeting with his counterparts in the other five divisions. My proposal was that the groups join to make a larger upfront investment and split the cost. In return, I would offer an aggressive price sheet that enabled the more mature divisions to move faster, while others could scale up over time. In the long run, the proposal would save them money and alleviate the pain of introducing the same initiative five different times. The difference it made to my deal? I literally added a zero to the original figure and grew my deal 10x. It would have been easy to take down the transaction, but I took a chance and pushed and it worked for me.

The enterprise-level proposal is another BAP success I've closed many times. I make it a rule to include an enterprise option whenever I deliver a quote to a serious prospect. Most companies are thinking small when they first approach a vendor, and the enterprise option is your opportunity to expand their thinking and define what's possible. By opening this door, you can begin shaping a final proposal that's more lucrative and ambitious—the very definition of the BAP. Why wait two or three years to sell the customer 40,000 units when you can make a convincing case for them to buy everything *now*? Generally, the enterprise option supports rapid growth and adoption of your product while providing maximum flexibility, and many companies are willing to pay a premium for this convenience. The enterprise proposal is a great way for you to flex your BAP muscles and take down some nice deals while you're learning this approach.

Now, the BAP that failed: I had been working with my contact at a financial services company on a project that we both believed lacked the proper funding and ambition to succeed. We collaborated to produce a further-reaching proposal we knew was a sure winner. Our new approach addressed a strategic objective around cost reduction that was very important to the SVP, and our business case included detailed financial projections demonstrating how we would save the company $400K *in the first year alone*. It was bulletproof. My contact scheduled time with his SVP to present our proposal, but at the last minute he got cold feet. "I'm only authorized to spend $200K," he told me, "and I don't know how the SVP will react to a proposal for three times that. I just can't do it." We ended up pursuing the smaller initiative for around $160K, but the win was bittersweet. All I could think about was the big one that got away.

I include the failed BAP story because it illustrates the mental hurdles that both you *and* the client will need to overcome to make the BAP successful. Winning with the BAP strategy requires patience, boldness, conviction, and the willingness to take a chance, but the payoff can be immense. Once you've established the right mindset and found the right client, you can start swinging for the fences. I'll tell you this: once you've had a taste of the big deals, you'll never want to settle for the small transactions again.

* GAME PREP *

Start by examining your own buying habits to profile the type of buyer that you are (bold, cautious, or impatient). Now think about how your buying profile influences your sales approach. Does your selling style reflect your profile as a buyer? Salespeople with a more cautious buying approach usually have the biggest challenge when it comes to adopting the BAP mindset, because it contradicts their fundamental beliefs: *I'm a safe buyer; I don't take risks; why should I expect a customer to buy this way?* If you're a bold buyer, you have a built-in advantage when it comes to succeeding with the BAP.

Understanding how you buy and how it influences your approach to sales is a critical step, and will give you insight into the steepness of your climb. Once you understand your profile, promise yourself to start taking the initiative and being more bold in your proposals. Next, think about your current deals, and which of these might lend itself to a BAP experiment. Although you may find the perfect deal right away, it's more likely that you'll need to use your influence to create the right conditions for the BAP. Here are some suggestions to get you started:

Read the situation: Not every sales situation lends itself to a BAP. Look for the following conditions: (1) a need that is underserved by a limited transaction, i.e. the prospect is thinking too small; (2) close alignment with a top strategic priority; (3) a sponsor with the right vision; (4) a compelling ROI that will justify a bigger purchase; and (5) the right economic conditions (they can find the money).

Tie the BAP into a strategic initiative: By nature, the BAP is a strategic engagement that will require time and resources. Companies don't bet big to solve department-level problems, but they'll invest heavily in projects that support strategic goals. (**#20: Solve Their Big Hairy Problem** discusses this in more detail).

Create the vision: The BAP is all about envisioning the future and taking bold steps to make it happen. You need to create this vision and make it real for your prospect. *Don't sell your product—sell the vision.*

Understand the bigger picture: What kind of growth does your client expect? Where do they want to be in a year, or two years? The BAP can make a compelling business case for a bigger upfront investment for clients anticipating steady growth.

Ally yourself with the visionary: The BAP usually doesn't resonate with corporate apparatchiks and pencil-pushers. Team up with the people who possess the same vision and can make things happen; they'll help you to position and sell your proposal.

Soften the ground: It's not in your best interest to surprise the client with a BAP. Socialize the idea first with people you trust, or ask them to co-develop the proposal with you. Their inside perspective can help you anticipate objections and create a pitch that hits all the right points.

Smash the "pilot" mindset: Companies are inherently risk-averse, and a majority of buyers want to run a pilot before they invest. Introduce a sense of urgency and push the client to buy now instead of running a pilot.

Have a "Plan B": Not every client will buy into your vision, so have a backup proposal. This may be your original deal or a scaled-down version of the BAP, but you don't want the BAP to be an all-or-nothing proposition. Take your shot, and if it doesn't work, take down the smaller transaction.

Make it a habit: If you try regularly to think bigger and look for BAP potential on every deal, you'll improve your chances of success and change your entire sales approach to sales for the better. THINK BIG.

* SHOWTIME *

Like any strategic proposal, the BAP is most effective when it's delivered in person. When you're face-to-face with the client, your enthusiasm and excitement is palpable, and make no mistake: you need to channel your inner P.T. Barnum to sell the vision and excite your audience. Meetings establish a level of gravity and intimacy that's entirely appropriate for a proposal of this magnitude, so do your best to get in front of the customer when you have the opportunity to present your BAP.

Start with the vision and why you believe your prospect should think BIG and pursue your recommended course of action. **Always sell the vision to get people excited and make sure it's backed up with numbers and a compelling business case.** Whenever possible, co-present with your sponsors and ask them to voice their opinions. Strong internal advocacy is crucial to gain support for the BAP, so draw upon this support and use it to your advantage. The reality is that executives will listen to you, but they *really* pay attention when someone on their own team makes the case.

Be prepared for questions, and don't be afraid to challenge the client if they continue to think small. Maintain your poise and confidence no matter what, because **your worst move is to present a bold vision and then meekly retreat when things get a bit bumpy**. When you believe your proposal is the right one for the customer, advocate this path with passion and show that you believe in what you're presenting. No customer will fault you for advocating a bold course of action that you sincerely believe will help them to meet their goals.

As with any pitch, you need to sell the decision-makers on your vision. You should know exactly which people in the room have the power, so tailor your presentation to them. Executives are paid to see the bigger picture and will be in a better position to understand the BAP. If you've prepared well, your sponsors have briefed you on the executive's hot buttons and you can incorporate these points into your pitch. Expect the BAP sales cycle to take a bit longer than a transactional deal, but nobody will mind a little extra time when your deal doubles (or more) in size.

Of course the real work begins when the customer signs the contract. BAPs are often larger and more complex sales that will involve multiple departments and stakeholders and hold special interest for the executives. **The client has bought into your grand vision, so you better make sure your company is in a position to deliver.** Failure to deliver on the BAP is unconscionable, so validate your proposal internally *before* it's presented to the customer.

Over time, you'll find yourself playing on a whole new level and delivering more strategic proposals to executive-level contacts. Big-game hunting has its rewards, and bigger revenue numbers and commission checks are foremost among them. THINK BIG and the BAP will help you succeed beyond your wildest dreams.

#17: Nail the Pilot

Today, every company wants to try before they buy. When you nail the pilot, you'll make the sale. This technique is all about running a flawless evaluation process that will set you up perfectly for the bigger deal.

Pilots. Evaluations. Proofs-of-concept. Whatever the term, if you're hearing these words more often from your prospects, you're not alone. For most companies selling in today's B2B marketplace, prospective customers are requesting hands-on evaluations of your product before they commit to buy.

There are powerful forces converging to perpetuate this growing trend: a sluggish global economy; greater aversion to risk; more informed buyers with greater access to data; and a shift in power as buyers assert themselves in the sales process. In the past, pilots were required only for new vendors selling technically complex or very expensive products and solutions. Today, pilots have become S.O.P. for almost every corporate purchase. At the end of the day, the burden is on you to prove your value *before* you're rewarded with the bigger deal.

This technique was developed through necessity while I was working for a West Coast-based software company. One day the CRO called me into his office to discuss a major problem. Our salesforce was running more pilots than ever, but less than half of these were converting into revenue. When we considered the time, effort and resources necessary to run a pilot, not to mention opportunity cost and lost revenue for those that failed to become deals, *our pilot failures were costing us more than $1M a year.*

The bottom line? We just couldn't nail the pilot.

The CRO asked me to figure this out, and I assembled a team and got to work. **Less than one year later, we were converting more than 90% of our pilots into signed deals.** What I'd discovered was that there was a much better way to run a pilot program, and our new approach helped us **double our success rate**. Previously, our pilots lacked structure; our engagement was haphazard; we let the prospect set the agenda; we lacked clear goals; and there was no agreement on next steps once the pilot concluded. Once we addressed these shortcomings, our win rates soared. We had discovered how to *nail the pilot every single time*, and the benefits were significant:

- **Better win rates**: In this example, our wins rates soared from 45% to 90%. I've implemented the improved pilot program at other companies and have seen similarly impressive results.
- **More revenue**: We signed bigger deals and we won more often. In one year we closed twice as many deals and grew deal size by 30%.
- **Competitive differentiator**: We shone while our competitors stumbled. Once we shared our system, buyers would dismiss our competition and run pilots exclusively with us.
- **More control**: We seized control of the sales process and dictated the terms of the sale.
- **Greater credibility**: Buyers were impressed with our execution and ability to run a disciplined process that delivered results.
- **Efficiency improvements:** These included reduced pilot-cycle times, better resource utilization and more accurate revenue forecasting.

* GAME PREP *

What's your company's attitude when it comes to pilots? Some companies have accepted pilots as a necessary step in their sales cycle, while others will press the salesforce to avoid them at all costs. In either case, **it's almost always the prospect that requests a pilot**. Few salespeople will enthusiastically offer up an evaluation as it extends the sales cycle and adds complexity to the deal. Regardless, you need to be prepared because you can be sure that your prospects will ask.

You are *always* the final decision-maker on whether or not you run a pilot with a prospect. Just because the prospect raises the possibility of a pilot doesn't mean that you have to agree. Your very first step in running a winning pilot is to determine whether the prospect is a good candidate for the pilot, and how likely they are to turn into a paying customer later. Before committing to any pilot, answer the following questions:

- Are the right conditions in place to run a successful pilot?
- Will I have access to the right personnel, business units and key decision makers?
- Are there clear and achievable business goals?
- Is there a tacit or stated agreement to purchase upon a successful conclusion?
- What's the potential payoff when we're successful?

The Pilot Questionnaire is a checklist that has been designed specifically to assist you in determining the fitness of a prospect for your pilot program. It can be filled out in a 30-minute discovery call with your prospect, and will become crucial to your planning and execution process.

Pilot Questionnaire ("PQ")

The PQ should be completed and internally reviewed before any commitment is made to initiate a pilot. The salesperson completes the PQ in collaboration with the prospect, and then presents it to an approval committee. Optimally, this committee includes a decision-maker from every group involved in the pilot process (sales, consulting, engineering), and its role is to approve pilots, enforce standards, and share responsibility for driving a successful outcome. No pilot may be undertaken without the committee's approval, and questionable prospects are either turned away or given conditions to meet before a pilot can be initiated. A PQ should contain the following information:

- **Stakeholders/Decision-makers**: Detail who the important stakeholders are, what role they'll play in the pilot, who makes the final decision, and who owns the budget.

- **Schedule/Timeline**: The expected timeline for the pilot, including end date, checkpoints, close meetings and other important events.
- **Success criteria**: What needs to happen for the prospect to declare the pilot a success? This is important, because all work in the pilot will be performed in the service of meeting the success criteria.
- **Use cases**: Use cases are real-life business scenarios that the prospect will use your product to address. What use cases does the prospect need to see to declare the pilot a success?
- **Business problems**: What are the specific business problems the prospect is trying to solve?
- **Action items/Responsibilities**: Definition of each task to be performed in the evaluation and who's responsible for doing it.
- **Financial**: Are you charging the prospect for the pilot, or is it free? This is a big decision and will depend on your market and buyers. Requiring prospects to have "skin in the game" can ensure that they're serious, but not all prospects have the means or desire to pay for a pilot.
- **Next steps**: What happens when the pilot is completed? Optimally, the prospect has agreed to make a purchase. Vague commitments on next steps are a red flag.
- **Risks/Unknowns**: Your internal perspective on the risks that may jeopardize a successful outcome. These risk factors are often raised by the committee once they've reviewed the PQ.

A completed PQ becomes a rapid assessment tool for you and your committee to determine if the pilot has a good shot at success and can be counted on to produce future revenue. **If the perceived risks outweigh the potential benefits or the prospect is vague on future commitments, you should not run the pilot.** Although it's hard to tell a prospect "No," this momentary sting is far less painful than investing energy in a pilot that fails. **Your ability to nail the pilot starts with accepting *only* the pilots you know you can win.**

Once you've made the decision to run the pilot, the hard work begins. At this point, you'll leverage the information captured in the PQ to develop the document that will govern the entire pilot process: the Pilot Charter.

Pilot Charter ("PC")

As you've already done most of the heavy lifting during the PQ phase to define stakeholders, responsibilities, timelines, use cases, business problems, success criteria, and next steps, the PC is simply a formal version of this document that you can share and validate with the prospect. The PC becomes the governing document for your project, and aligns everybody behind a common vision and the steps required to reach a successful outcome. A comprehensive PC is important in that it establishes the right expectations and clearly states the scope of the pilot, helping you to avoid "mission creep" if the prospect starts demanding more once you've begun.

Successful pilots are highly structured, high-touch program in which your resources are working to prove the success criteria and use cases that the prospect has indicated must be fulfilled for the pilot to be a declared a success. You never want to just set the customer loose with your product and hope for the best, and this is why the PC is so important in your planning process. The completed PC will help you execute and become a roadmap for your success.

* SHOWTIME *

At this point, you've (1) qualified your prospect for the pilot, (2) detailed all relevant information and received buy-in from your committee, and (3) created the charter document and received buy-in from your client. How you execute will now determine the ultimate success of your pilot. The pilot cadence is a methodical, step-by-step process consisting of three steps: Define, Demonstrate, and Validate.

- **Define**: Proof points or use cases that the prospect needs to see (as defined in the pilot charter).
- **Demonstrate**: A demonstration of exactly how your product meets the defined proof points and use cases.
- **Validate**: The prospect's acknowledgement that you've met the proof point before moving on to the next one.

My pilot team is small; in most cases it's just me and my sales engineer. He usually takes the lead on running the pilot, and this is helpful for two reasons. First, he's a product expert and brings knowledge and credibility to the engagement. Second, as SE, he's there solely to help and takes no role in "selling" the prospect. He's not the focus of any negative or stressful vibes that a prospect may display when in a business meeting (that's my role). He's viewed as a peer, and can therefore be privy to casual asides and inside information that the prospect wouldn't necessarily share with me. My SE, of course, shares *all* information with me, and this helps us to make adjustments and fine-tune our strategy.

The SE's mandate is simple: work through the Define/Demonstrate/Validate process with the prospect until they've agreed that we've met their success criteria. Most pilots focus on five or six proof points and last from two to three weeks. During this time, the SE acts as Sherpa, guiding the prospect up the mountain until all of their proof points are demonstrated and validated. At this point, it's time for the salesperson to re-engage and nudge the prospect toward a purchase. Because the PC already spells out next steps, this task should be a formality. To seal the deal, I use two of my favorite close techniques: **advocate selling** and **the close meeting**.

Advocate Selling

The purpose of advocate selling is to create internal advocacy for your product by developing strong champions who (a) want your product, and (b) are willing to push the decision-makers to buy it. The SE cultivates and nurtures potential advocates during the pilot process, and the goal is to make them feel a sense of ownership in your product. When you make people *want* your product, they'll go to bat for you with their executives and steer you through the Legal and Procurement minefields.

Advocates can become your secret weapons in the pilot process, and their support will make a huge difference when it comes to securing budget and obtaining the necessary approvals for a purchase. While advocate selling can work in any sales cycle, it's especially powerful in the pilot process because you've *shown* the advocate how you're going to help them and *convinced* them that you're the right solution. Once they've made up their mind, you've got them.

The Close Meeting

The close meeting is a formal wrap-up of the pilot and a transition into the next phase of your relationship. Your advocates and the decision-maker(s) must attend this meeting, and your job is to validate the success of the pilot and ASK for the business. As you've clearly laid out next steps in the PC, it's a natural conversation that simply marks the evolution of the buyer from *prospect* to *customer*.

Here's an example of how advocate selling and the close meeting can converge to produce spectacular results:

> *We were concluding a competitive, three-month pilot with a Fortune 500 company. We'd built advocacy among the evaluation team, and defined a date for the close meeting in the pilot charter. Our plan was to present the results, walk the executive through the important use cases and ask for their commitment to buy. Only it wouldn't be us presenting the results and asking for the commitment.*

> *Because we'd spent considerable time training our advocate to be proficient with our solution, he was able to guide the executive through every use case. Without speaking a word, we had achieved instant credibility and built the business case for our solution. The following week, we were back in to meet with the client. . . only this time it was to sign a deal worth several hundred thousand dollars.*

It's an indisputable fact that every salesperson would rather make the sale than run a pilot, but the rules have changed, and salespeople need to adapt. Pilots are here to stay, and your business better make sure it's damn good at running comprehensive, hands-on evaluations with prospects because your revenue targets may depend on it. Perfecting the pilot process is one of those rare steps that will generate an almost immediate ROI for sales organizations, and this makes it important. When you follow this program, you're distilling the pilot process down to a science and positioning yourself to execute flawlessly, and in this way you're sure to **Nail the Pilot** every time.

#18: ASK for the Business

Never underestimate the power of the ASK. Asking for a client's business is one of the simplest and most powerful actions you can take. You'll accelerate your deals and knock down the obstacles standing between you and a signed contract.

The ASK is as straightforward as it sounds. It's the act of actually asking a prospective customer for their business. It's a trial close on steroids, and you win whether the prospect says Yes or No. Think about this for a moment: how many sales techniques offer a no-lose proposition? With such a powerful weapon in their arsenal, it amazes me that so many salespeople struggle with the simple act of asking a prospect to buy from them.

Your top producers, of course, have mastered the art of the ASK and use it to accelerate their deals, improve close ratios and weed out the tire-kickers who have no intention of buying. **Here's the secret of the ASK: it's not just about securing the commitment, but also drawing out the issues that might prevent you from closing the deal.** It's a gutsy move, and when you lay your cards on the table you're inviting your prospect to do the same.

The possible outcomes are: (1) a commitment to buy, (2) a list of issues that need to be fixed to win the business, or (3) a clear indication that the prospect isn't buying. The ASK will either map your route to a signed contract or disqualify the prospect, freeing you up to pursue more promising opportunities. You win in every case, and this is what makes the ASK so compelling.

It's been noted that B2B sales cycles often feel like pre-scripted theatre in which each party knows and plays a role. You're the dutiful sales professional responsible for pitching your solution and answering your prospect's questions. The prospect, in turn, plays his cards close to the vest, revealing just enough information to get you started. You both know not to introduce money or the specter of commitment into the conversation until the buyer is good and ready. This kind of thinking is outdated, and prevents you from reaching your goals faster and with less static.

One straitjacket that many salespeople slip on—all too willingly—is the premise that every aspect of their product needs to be proven beyond a shadow of a doubt before they can ASK for the business. I fundamentally disagree with this assertion and contend that salespeople do themselves a big disservice by not asking sooner for a prospect's business. I've seen firsthand the difficulty that many professional salespeople have with the ASK conversation, and it blows my mind. You would *think* that people go into sales because they're comfortable asking for commitments and money, but this one simple act seems to generate significant angst.

There are many reasons for this. People hold out absurd hope for the impossible, and the ASK opens you up for a resounding "No" if you haven't done your job. Relationship-based salespeople don't want to jeopardize the delicate balance they've achieved by introducing the nasty concept of money. Many salespeople are happy to do the sales kabuki dance and wait until the prospect initiates a buy conversation. Show me a million different sales cycles and I'll show you a million reasons why salespeople avoid ASKing for the business.

This technique requires confidence, timing and hard work to move the prospect to the point where the ASK will be successful. A number of the companies I interviewed for this book actually understood the ASK better than the reps trying to sell them, and one customer told me that he was compelled to take matters into his own hands when the rep's reluctance began to slow him down:

"I felt bad, like I was wasting their time," he confided in me, "but the sales rep waited so long that I finally brought it up myself. My diligence was done and I needed to have the solution in place to meet our internal timeline, but the guy just kept insisting on scheduling demos and trying to prove what I was already sold on. Finally, I told him to write up a contract and send it to me."

Imagine that—a customer prodding their salesperson to hurry up and close the deal! *Amazing*. Make a commitment right now to master the ASK and you'll never be "that" sales rep.

* GAME PREP *

Theoretically, the ASK can be applied to any prospect at any stage in the sales cycle. That said, success rates tend to rise when you have *earned* the right to ASK and given the prospect every reason to say "Yes." The brief checklist below is a reality check before you ASK a prospect for their business. Your most likely candidates will meet all four criteria:

1. The prospect intends to buy and believes your product will meet their needs.
2. There's money available for the purchase.
3. There's a sense of urgency.
4. There's authority to buy (i.e., someone who can say "Yes").

Trust your instincts when considering whether or not to ASK a prospect for their business. If you honestly believe that the prospect thinks you're the right solution and they have the means to buy your product, go ahead and ASK. If you have not yet established their belief in your solution, springing the ASK on them won't work and may actually complicate your efforts to close them later. Because you've been applying other trial closes throughout your sales cycle (like a good salesperson should), you'll have a sense of how your client perceives your company and their readiness to make a bigger commitment. In cases where a prospect stands to see massive financial gain with your products or has a pressing sense of urgency (see **#4: Go Looking for Trouble**), you can press this leverage earlier with the buyer to secure the deal.

Who do you approach with the ASK? **Your most effective ASK conversation will be with the decision-maker or budget holder. You're asking for commitment, and want to be speaking with the person authorized to make it.** Executives tend to be more blunt, and usually won't hesitate to tell you what you need to do to sell them. Champions and sponsors make good sounding boards before you approach the executive, and can give their opinion on the outcome and coach you on the most effective delivery. As with many other opportunities to pitch the client, you may only get one shot at the ASK conversation, so choose your timing and audience wisely.

* SHOWTIME *

You have two primary objectives with the ASK conversation:

1. Secure a commitment to buy from the prospect.
2. Identify remaining obstacles that stand in your way (if any).

Here's a sample script for the ASK conversation:

> *"Mark, I've enjoyed working with your team over the past few months to understand your needs and how my product will meet them. I'm confident that my company can help you, and based on our conversations it sounds as though you feel the same way. You've indicated that you're under pressure to get started quickly, and we both know how long it can take to move a contract through Procurement. With your OK, I'd like to begin preparing final paperwork for your approval."*

The ASK can be subtle or overt. My preferred approach is to ask the customer for their business *without* actually asking the customer for their business. This means that I don't just blurt out "Buy from me Mark." Instead, I ask for his permission to take a step that we both know leads to a signed contract. It's a matter of style, and there are situations where the direct approach is more effective. It completely depends on the client and their particular circumstances, so actively experiment with different approaches to find one that works for you.

The hardest part of the ASK conversation is preparing yourself for a negative reply, but even this becomes easier when you realize that any response will move you closer to your goal. Let's dissect both the positive and negative responses that Mark may give to my hypothetical ASK:

Response #1:

> *MARK: Jonathan, we do feel the same way and appreciate your work with us. Please write up the paperwork and I will review it with my team before we submit it to Legal and Procurement.*

Wow—this is the stuff that dreams are made of. Congratulations; you're well on your way to closing the deal.

Or,

Response #2:

> *MARK: Jonathan, we like your solution and feel as though it meets most of our needs. But we're not yet ready to make a commitment.*

If the customer had responded with a flat-out "No," at least I'd know where I stood, and I could move on to more promising opportunities. In this case, the answer is not "No" but "Not yet." I can live with this, and now my task is to uncover the issues blocking my path to a sale. Here's the best follow-up question I can ask:

> *ME: What's preventing you from making a commitment at this point?*
>
> *MARK: I still don't understand how to configure your product to meet our business model. Also, our Security team has raised several concerns that need to be addressed before they will sign off on your platform.*

Bingo. With this simple line of questioning, I've now uncovered the issues that need to be addressed before Mark will buy. I'm already beginning to formulate a plan and identify the resources I'll need to address these objections. Technique **#7: The Tip of the Iceberg** teaches us that objections are usually masking more serious problems, and this is where I use a trial close to test whether or not Mark's objections are the real issues in my deal:

ME: I understand, and thank you for sharing this with me. **Let me ask you this Mark: If I'm able to resolve these issues to your satisfaction over the next two weeks, will you give me a commitment to buy?** *In turn, you have my promise to do everything I possibly can to address these issues for you.*

If the client is serious about buying and the objections they raised are the *true* roadblocks, they should have no problem making this commitment. If they won't commit, you need to dig deeper and uncover the *real* issues behind their objections. With this response, you're also asking the customer for permission to work on resolving their issues, because resolution will require time and effort on both sides. **You might think twice about increasing your level of commitment if the prospect's unwilling to reciprocate.**

A salesperson I respect very much took her ASK technique to an entirely new level. She would ask the prospect for their business, and when objections were raised, her response was, "If I can make that issue go away, will you buy?" She could run through as many as five objections before she finally wore the prospect down and secured a commitment. We called it "deal by exhaustion." It became a cornerstone of her approach and a big reason why she maintained a permanent perch atop the leaderboard. This tactic may not be everyone's cup of tea, but it certainly worked for her.

It's hard to think of any question quite as powerful as the ASK when wielded by a capable sales professional. This simple request gives you a reality check on your deal and a roadmap to close. It accelerates your sales cycle. It reveals any problems standing between you and a signed contract, and grants you permission to fix these problems. It separates the serious buyers from the pretenders. Master the art of the ASK and you'll elevate your game, strengthen your sales foundation, and put yourself in a position to drive more sales and better results.

#19: A Taste of Honey

You know that your products are irresistible. Give your prospects a little taste to get them hooked and you'll have a customer for life.

In their article "The End of Solution Sales," the authors of the Challenger Sales methodology quote a study of more than 1,400 B2B customers by the Corporate Executive Board. The study asserts that, on average, **almost 60% of a purchasing decision is made *before* the customer ever has a conversation with a supplier.**

I find this statistic fascinating because it points to a fundamental shift in the dynamics of the B2B marketplace. The Internet has empowered buyers by giving them unprecedented access to data and more confidence to diagnose their own problems. By the time a buyer calls you, chances are that they already have a thorough understanding of your market, competitors, pricing and reputation. It's also likely that they've engaged several vendors, and will leverage their research to play you off against each other and to drive down the price-point. This buying behavior is what one would normally see in commodity markets, and creates a nightmare sales scenario in which every deal is a competitive dogfight in which cost is all that matters.

If you believe that 60% of the sales cycle is beyond your control, it's imperative for you to differentiate and show massive value in the remaining 40%. This can only be accomplished when you seize control of the sales cycle and pull the buyer in. Your best bet to engage the buyer is by giving them a little taste of your product or service, and then sign them to a deal while the sweetness still lingers.

While I call this technique **A Taste of Honey**, my less politically-correct colleagues refer to it as the "crack principle." The insinuation is that your product is addictive, and by offering prospective customers a free sample you can get them hooked and create a customer for life. Another example comes from a dog breeder I know, who boosts sales by allowing families shopping for a puppy to take their favorite dog home for the weekend. As you might expect, nine times out of ten the family ends up buying the dog.

You know how good your products and services are, and that they'll deliver massive value to the prospect. Your challenge is to convince the prospect that you're the right solution when you only have 40% of the sales cycle to do so. There's no better way to drive results than creating a product experience that gives the buyer a little **Taste of Honey** and leaves them wanting more. You'll get them hooked and make the sale every time.

* GAME PREP *

From guided evaluations to pilots, proofs-of-concept, and free consulting, the concept of allowing customers to sample your offerings is not new. *That's because it works.* Your goal is to design novel ways to engage your prospects and draw them in, so consider the following factors when designing your approach:

- **Solution & Market:** Do your offerings lend themselves to a limited trial? Would your buyers embrace this type of offer? If the answer is Yes, this program will help you win.
- **Paid vs. Free:** Many evaluations are complimentary, but some companies ask the prospect to put skin in the game with a small investment to cover costs. In some cases, this approach can even create a new revenue stream.
- **Experience:** The best evaluations highlight your strengths and become templates for future engagements. No need to reinvent the wheel each time. Consider how to deliver the best possible experience for your prospect and set the stage for a sale.
- **Engagement depth:** The best programs offer just a taste without revealing everything. (There are some secrets that you only share with customers.) A successful evaluation shows the prospect *just enough* to secure the business.
- **Momentum:** A best-case scenario is that prospects will leverage the work they've done in the evaluation when they

become a customer. Avoid "throwaway" trials that provide no lasting value.

- **Resources:** Clearly define what resources are required to run an evaluation program, and budget people's time for this important pre-sales activity. This often means working across multiple departments, so secure buy-in from the right people in your organization.
- **Timeframe:** How long does the evaluation last? How do you ensure that this step won't unnecessarily extend your sales cycle?
- **Support:** The days of setting prospects loose with your product are over. You need to be a Sherpa guiding them to the summit, not a phone-in techie. Provide training and schedule regular checkpoints to answer their questions and monitor progress.

Because an evaluation program requires time and resources, **it should only be offered to the prospects most likely to buy from you**. If you believe an evaluation will tip the scales in your favor and make the difference in your sales cycle, I'd consider this a qualified prospect. Once you're sure, make certain what you're offering aligns with the prospect's needs. If they can use your product in a live environment with their own data, it's a home run resulting in an easy transition once they buy. **If the prospect is using your product to help their business, it's hard for them to turn it off and walk away.** Rather than simply activating the client in a test environment, look for ways to integrate your product into their daily routine and make them depend on it. There's no surer formula to make the sale.

Although both programs share some common characteristics, this technique differs from **#17: Nail the Pilot** in that *you're* initiating a limited trial to get the prospect engaged and secure their commitment. Unlike formal pilots that tend to be more structured and lengthy, these programs are designed to be relatively quick and lightweight—but still impactful enough to win the business. You *want* to have these sales tools available to you because they're your most powerful option for clients considering competitive options or unsure of the value they'll see with your solution.

As it will be *you* who raises the prospect of a limited trial, here's a sample script to get you started:

> *"Sheila, I know you're interested in my product and anxious to start using it. We usually accomplish this through a 2-week, hands-on evaluation process that will validate your proof points and let you fully experience how the product works. Once you fall in love with it, we can talk about making you a customer. Agreed?"*

You should review **#17: Nail the Pilot** because the best practices it lays out for running an evaluation will also apply to your trial programs. Briefly, your most successful trials are going to (1) achieve specific, pre-defined objectives, (2) build goodwill and relationships with your client, and (3) be managed closely by you and your team to ensure a successful outcome.

* SHOWTIME *

There's plenty of room for creativity when designing these programs. Below are five examples that I've seen deployed with great success. Think about how these approaches might work for you:

- A product company allows prospective customers to use their products free-of-charge for three weeks. The vendor provides a brief training session and videos at kickoff, and schedules weekly checkpoints for Q&A. *Seventy percent of prospects in this program eventually convert into paying customers.*
- A consulting firm asks a prospect to submit three questions that are currently perplexing their business. The firm goes to work on these questions and returns with an in-depth study and customized recommendations. The prospect gains a valuable new perspective and the consultant showcases their abilities and expertise.
- A company offers a 1-day "boot camp" at their office for senior executives, during which they're immersed in the company's methodology and framework. It's a full day of

valuable executive networking and learning while the vendor builds bridges with important decision-makers.

- A software company runs a half-day "conference-room pilot" that immerses potential clients in the software platform. Less resource-intensive than a multi-week pilot, these engagements are a competitive differentiator, drive faster buy decisions, and enable multiple stakeholders to get hands-on with the product.

- A consulting firm offers a custom trial of their services in the form of a 4-6 week engagement at an aggressive price point. A seasoned consultant leads the project, but prospects are given only brief access to the senior partners and full resources of the firm. When the trial ends, most prospects are anxious to continue the work they've started *and* gain access to the senior partners.

#20: Solve Their Big Hairy Problem

The Big Hairy Problem ("BHP") is what keeps your clients awake at night. Solve it for them and you'll be rewarded with bigger deals and revered as a strategic partner.

Did you ever wonder what busy executives actually spend their days doing? Chances are, much of their time is focused on solving the BHPs that plague every business. By definition, BHPs are the serious issues that can threaten the very existence of an organization. As a result, they cascade down from senior management to every department and every employee in the company. **To use an old sales cliché, the BHP is the problem that keeps your clients awake at night**. When you can convince the client that you're part of the solution to their BHP, you'll make the sale every time.

It's common for salespeople to be brought in to help specific groups solve department-level problems. This is great, but also generates a transactional sale. **But when you can identify an enterprise-level challenge and become part of the solution, it's a game-changer.** Since it's standard practice for companies to throw money and resources at the BHP in a desperate attempt to find answers, their generosity can be your windfall. The BHP may be right out in the open or require some digging on your part, but believe me, it exists. No business runs perfectly, and every company has major challenges that it needs to solve.

A BHP example: I was calling on a company that had just acquired one of their major competitors. Through conversations with my contacts, I found out that the transition had been rocky, and senior management was very concerned about cultural and operational issues that had arisen from the merger. People were reporting to two (or more) bosses, entering the same data in three systems, and taking four times as long to complete basic tasks. Morale was suffering greatly, and management feared that this frustration would cause good people to walk out the door. This conundrum became their BHP.

This acquisition was a huge event for the parent company, and a failure to make it work would be catastrophic for the business. The CEO stated that fixing the BHP was to be *everyone's* top priority. At the time, I was running a sales cycle with one of the divisions, and it was frustrating because preoccupation with the BHP kept delaying my deal. As I learned more about the BHP, I had an idea: I would shift my tactics and recast my product as a solution to the BHP. When I was ready, I asked my contact to pull the right players together and stood up to address them:

> *"I recently became aware of the challenges that your company is having trying to assimilate your competitor's culture and technology with your own. I understand this is a high-priority issue for the CEO, and that each department has been asked to play a part in solving it. Since we've been focusing on a narrower objective, you may not even be aware that my technology can help address this challenge. I'd like to take the first 30 minutes of our meeting and show you how."*

Two hours later, we were still discussing my ideas. At one point, an executive excused himself only to reappear with two of his colleagues, both of whom stayed for the entire meeting. Not only did I build support for my proposal, I met several new executives and shifted the conversation in a more strategic direction. *All of this happened because I'd proven that I could help them solve the BHP*. Within 30 days we signed a deal that had grown in scope and become quite a bit larger than my original transaction. By becoming part of the BHP solution, I was able to sign a bigger deal and transcend my vendor role to become a more strategic partner in the customer's eyes.

This is the beauty of helping your customers solve the BHP: **it's a real opportunity to grow your deal, develop executive relationships, and elevate your status from vendor to strategic partner.** The BHP is your ticket to the executive suite, and with their support you'll have the money and resources you need to make sure your proposed solution works. While transactional reps hit singles and doubles, elite athletes hit home runs, and solving the BHP can be a home run for you. Similar to **#16: The Big**

Audacious Proposal, solving a company's BHP is one more way for you to burnish your reputation and propel yourself to the top of the leaderboard.

Finding and understanding the BHP is your first step, and this is accomplished through research and conversations with your client. When you know what you're dealing with, you can creatively map your solution to the problem. Finally, you need to build a business case that convinces the client that you're the solution they've been searching for. The end result is a fast-moving deal at a premium price-point that also gives you a real opportunity to create a more strategic partnership with your client.

* GAME PREP *

So what exactly is a BHP? Here's a list of some circumstances, events, and conditions that can create a BHP:

- Issues arising from a merger or acquisition
- Significant new competitive threat
- Disruption in their market
- Growth and/or profitability challenges
- Declining market share
- Major product miss or recall
- Highly-visible PR disaster
- Layoffs and executive departures

Unless you read about a company's BHP in the news, you're most likely to uncover it through conversations with their employees and executives in particular. While the BHP is a pressing problem for everyone, it's going to be top-of-mind with the executives. Your strategy is to fan out across multiple business units and have as many executive conversations as you can. The questions below are specifically designed to pinpoint the BHP, and should be used as part of your discovery process:

- What's the one big problem that would prompt you to buy today if I could help you solve it?
- What are the big issues your company is wrestling with today, and what is the potential payoff if you solve them?

- Will our work together further any high-level strategic initiatives or solve any other problems important to your executive team?
- What are the company's strategic goals for the next 12 months? Do you believe my solution could help you address any of these?
- Do you see any other applications for my product at your company?
- What are your CEO's top priorities?
- What are the most pressing issues for your department/division?
- What's holding your company back from reaching your (revenue/profit/growth) goals?
- We've resolved how my product is going to help you solve your (specific business) problems. What are the other big issues are keeping you up at night?

As you can see, this line of questioning is more suited for a senior person paid to think strategically than a line-level manager focused on their small slice of the business. Listen for words like *growth, profitability, priority, strategy* and *competitive threat,* as these often signify that you're getting close to the BHP.

If you're working at a departmental level, think about the business problems you've been engaged to solve. In my earlier example, I was brought in to solve a more limited problem that was still a symptom of the much larger malady—the struggling acquisition. Addressing the BHP was as simple as scaling up my solution to address the same problem at a higher level. When you believe you've found the BHP, validate your hunch with your contacts to ensure that you're on-target, and then begin developing your proposal to address the BHP and win the business.

* SHOWTIME *

Once you've found and validated the BHP, you're ready to create a proposal. **You can pitch your usual contacts, but I'd recommend pitching the executive**. Your message is strategic, and needs to be communicated to someone thinking at this level. Plus, most executives will have a personal stake in solving the

BHP, making them more receptive to your message. When you deliver your pitch, demonstrate that you understand the problem first and then present your solution—not just raw ideas. You want the client to be able to say "Yes" and get started immediately, so it's worth taking the time to create a plan of action that enables both of your to move with the appropriate degree of urgency. Consider this abridged BHP pitch that I recently delivered to a client:

> *"Ms. VP: As you know, I've been working with the Strategy team in Division A to help them do a better job cascading strategic goals down to the rest of the organization. Your CEO just gave an interview in which she stated that the biggest challenge your company faces is the failure to execute on its strategic goals. Rather than simply solving this problem for a single division, I propose that we make this a corporate-wide initiative. In this way, I believe we can double your goal-achievement percentages next year.*
>
> *Since Division A has a head start, we can deploy them first as a model for the other divisions as they ramp up over the next six months. I've put together an initial pricing proposal and deployment schedule for your approval. I can also set up a call with two references who have both seen the 50% uptick that I believe I can deliver for you."*

So what have I done here? I've leveraged my existing work with Division A to establish credibility and build a sense of momentum. I've demonstrated that I understand their challenge, and point to their CEO's statements as proof of its importance. I've set targets and highlighted results. I've proposed a course of action that will form the basis for our deployment. Finally, I've showcased my experience solving this problem for others, and offered up two customers as proof. *This* is how you stage and deliver the BHP pitch.

Once your engagement begins, the pressure is on you to deliver. While the BHP offers significant upside from a sales standpoint, the fallout can be disastrous if you take on a company's BHP and fail. **No salesperson wants to be the one who boldly promises**

results for the biggest problem his client faces and then fails to deliver. Before you propose to solve the BHP, present your ideas internally to your manager and extended sales and support teams. Let them poke holes in it, debate risks and verify that your outcome is achievable. This internal checkpoint is your insurance policy for future success, and may save you the pain of a very difficult conversation with a disappointed client.

Much like **#16: The Big Audacious Proposal** and **#3: Three New Ideas**, the BHP is a technique designed to drive much bigger deals at a more strategic level with clients. This is where the big dogs play; the sales reps consistently at the top of the leaderboard are always searching for the client's BHP so they can solve it. I have no problem whatsoever with transactional or inside sales; every organization needs singles and doubles to keep the lights on. But solving the BHP is a home run, and deals like this will propel you to a higher level in your career. *Always* keep your antennae extended for the BHP and be bold in seeking to solve it, because to the victor go the spoils.

#21: Let's Make a Deal

Learn what your prospects value most, and then make them an offer they can't refuse.

What's the first word that pops into your head when I say the word "incentive"? If you're answer is "discount," you're not alone. Cutting prices to drive sales certainly occupies a time-honored place in the Incentive Hall of Fame, because everyone likes to save money. Buyers, however, are motivated by more than just money, and your challenge (and reward) lies in discovering what a potential buyer truly values, and then creating the right offer that will prompt them to action.

While the terms "incentive" and "promotion" are often used interchangeably, the basic premise is the same: a targeted offer designed to accelerate the sales cycle and secure a commitment from the client to buy on a timeline favorable to you. While incentives are typically introduced to drive a pending deal to closure, they can also be used as a trial close to determine the seriousness of a potential buyer.

Optimally, the incentive and offer are customized to the specific needs of the buyer. I've never been a fan of "one-size-fits-all" promotions that unimaginative sales managers insist on running to jump-start slow quarters. **Your best strategy when designing promotions is to match the offer to the buyer.** The customers I interviewed for this book were nearly unanimous in their agreement on this point: *Show me that you listened and responded to my needs,* one customer told me, *and you'll get my business.*

Your company is sure to have a track record with incentives, so don't reinvent the wheel. Start by asking around your company to find out what kind of promotions have worked in the past and might also work for you. Even your competition can have good ideas, and I'll give you an example: my company was desperate to generate more "at bats" with prospects. We'd seen a decline in the number of inbound leads and we were losing deals to the competition, yet nobody knew why. We started by researching our closest competitors and their go-to-market strategy. What we discovered was that our biggest competitor was running a promotion for new customers that deferred all payments for six months or until the customer could see tangible results. If results didn't meet their expectations, the customer didn't need to pay.

Wow. Talk about standing behind your value proposition and sharing risk with the customer! While most executives would write this radical promotion off as financial suicide, our competitor had leveraged it to close several millions of dollars in new business and shut us out.

How? They understood the market and acknowledged a glaring reality: executives wanted to see results *before* they made a big investment, and they weren't willing to spend lots of money without solid proof. Although our competitor's products were no better than our own, they had made it much easier for customers to buy because their offer spoke directly to the customer's pain. We made some adjustments to our model, but the damage was done, and it was hard for us to recover from this downturn in our business.

Here are three factors every company should consider first when designing an intelligent incentive program:

- **Perception of value:** Whether it's cost savings, favorable payment terms or risk mitigation, you need to offer something that the prospect will see as valuable. Find out what they value most and make this the centerpiece of your offer.
- **Market specifics:** You know your market better than anyone. What will your prospects respond to? In my example, the buyers valued risk mitigation above saving a few bucks. Put yourself in their shoes to design incentives that will prompt them to action.
- **Urgency:** Incentives lose their punch when the prospect knows that you'll offer it again if they fail to move.

Incentives should be time-based and push the prospect to buy on *your* timeline.

It's worth noting that although the competitor from my previous example was charging higher fees than anyone else, I'd be willing to bet that both sides felt as though they got their money's worth. That's the beauty of a well-designed incentive; you get the deal and the prospect gets something they value. It's a winning strategy for everybody.

* GAME PREP *

Although most people will need management's OK to make a special offer, the creative process should begin with you: the account owner. You're closest to the prospect, you understand their needs, and you're ultimately responsible for results. Start by understanding your boundaries and the space you have to maneuver within the sales organization. If your company "gets" it, you'll be empowered to do whatever it takes to win the deal. Incentives also need to be applied strategically, as they lose their impact when they're thrown about like candy from a Mardi Gras float. Abuse incentives and your customers will begin to expect special terms for every transaction. The perception of exclusivity and the certainty that you're making a one-time, buy-now-or-it's-gone offer is what makes incentives so effective in closing business.

The following is a list of common incentives offered by sellers:

- Favorable or delayed payment terms
- Extended contract terms (13-month term instead of 12-months)
- Discounts
- Shared risk ("skin in the game")
- Guarantees
- Free upgrades
- Supplemental or add-on products
- Free training
- Access to power (executives)
- Consulting sessions

- Publicity, press release or case study
- Speaking opportunities
- Participation in a webinar
- Inclusion in certain groups (pre-release beta testers)
- Access to your network of customers for calls and site visits

The best incentives will (1) speak directly to the client's needs, and (2) introduce a sense of urgency that leads to action. My own personal strategy is to approach my prospects with *two* offers in my pocket, just in case the first offer misses the mark. It can never hurt to have a "Plan B" ready to go in case you need it. Incentives work best when they're used strategically to control the ebb and flow of the sales cycle and prompt customer action when *you're* ready to close the business. Plus, your client will know that you're ready to make a deal, and that's when the real fun begins.

* SHOWTIME *

When is the right time to make your offer? I use the 50% rule, meaning that I present an offer when I perceive my chances of closing a deal to be fifty percent or higher. At this juncture in the sales cycle, my goal is a verbal commitment to buy. If you're still early in the sales cycle, incentives can make you seem desperate and even cause more harm than good, so use good judgment.

Unlike other sales pitches discussed in this book, incentives don't necessarily need to be presented to executives. In fact, your day-to-day contact can provide feedback and give you their initial impressions before they take your offer to the decision-makers. Your contacts know what motivates people in their organization, and their feedback can send you in new (and more fruitful) directions before you finalize your offer. Collaboration can be key in designing the right incentive for your clients, so solicit input to make sure you get it right.

Incentives can also be powerful when used as part of a trial close:

"Hello, Jim, I'm calling because my manager has empowered me to make you an offer to bring our pending business to a

close. It's only good for the current quarter, so let me share the specifics and let's see if it hits the right notes for you."

Every salesperson grows to love trial closes, so here's another variation of the same message:

"Hello, Jim, I know we've spoken in the past about your desire to purchase our latest product upgrade. I've racked my brain and have come up with a deal to get you this upgrade at a significant discount, assuming we can sign the deal this month. Let's connect as soon as possible to walk through the specifics."

When Jim and I talk, he'll either accept my offer or give me the reasons why he can't buy now. Either way, I win, because I've created the right conditions for Jim to say "Yes" and given him incentive to move. I may have to fall back on Plan B or even Plan C, but I've opened up a buying discussion, and this is exactly the conversation I want to have.

Incentives can help you to accelerate the buying conversation, give lagging prospects a push, and weed out the pretenders. Incentives are an important facet of creative dealmaking and show that you and your company are serious players who are willing to negotiate. When you understand what motivates your buyers, you can design the right incentives to push their hot buttons and drive results. Believe me: your clients *will* respond.

#22: Plan to Close with a Close Plan

Once the customer says "Yes," the hard work really begins. By detailing every step in your process and by making both sides accountable for a signed contract, the Close Plan ensures that your deal gets done.

Over a long career selling software to businesses, I've found the Close Plan ("CP") to be one of the most effective—yet consistently underutilized—resources in the sales arsenal. **Once you've received a verbal commitment to buy from the prospect, the creation of a CP should be a mandatory next step on every deal.** The path from verbal commitment to signed contract can be long and treacherous, and many of the greatest sales failures I've seen occur when salespeople think the deal's won and take their foot off the accelerator. *Big mistake.* By working with the prospect to establish a timeline with every last step clearly defined, you minimize risk and create accountability on both sides to produce a signed contract.

Let's face it—when you're in sales, the odds are stacked against you. Prospects come up with a million reasons why a sale is stalling, and **you never really know what maneuvering is taking place behind the scenes**. Competitors keep calling and want to steal your business. Key people resign, get fired or assume new responsibilities in the middle of negotiations. Procurement can take forever, and budget mysteriously disappears. Corporate restructuring or executive shake-ups can put everything on hold. *The reality is that your deal is in jeopardy until the contract is signed, and some of the hardest work in the sales cycle begins when the prospect says "Yes."*

Most sales organizations consider a deal to be in the bag when they receive a verbal commitment from the client, and losing these "sure things" is tough. Everyone feels the sting; leadership and support teams, investors, and the many others who plan their future activities based on sales commitments and anticipated revenue. There is nothing worse than a committed deal evaporating into nothingness, and this is why the verbal commitment represents a critical juncture in your deal. You need to validate every assumption, ask questions, search for blind spots, and hold the customer's hand as you wind through their buying process. The CP does all of this, and it will become your trusted guide through the rocky and uncertain terrain of corporate procurement.

By definition, the CP is a detailed roadmap of all the remaining steps that need to occur for the customer to sign your contract. It answers the *Who*, *What*, *When* and *How* questions about your deal, and enables you to micromanage the entire close process. It's advantages are clear:

- **Better intelligence:** Rather than guess and hope, you *know*: what specific steps need to happen and by when, and whom to hold accountable if deadlines are missed.
- **Mutual agreement:** The CP is developed in collaboration with the prospect and agreed to by both parties. By validating the CP, the prospect is endorsing the purchase and offering to help you close the deal.
- **Accountability:** At its core, the CP is a trial close. By clearly binding tasks to people, it creates accountability for their completion.
- **Predictability & Credibility:** When you can present a CP that walks your manager through every remaining step in your deal, they'll believe your forecast. CPs make close dates more predictable and enhance your credibility with management.
- **Risk mitigation:** Every deal is at risk until the contract is signed, and this is especially true in the period between verbal commitment and signature. A roadmap through this difficult period reduces the chance of nasty surprises and other bumps that can derail your deal.
- **Roadmap to close:** Every company's buying process is complex and unique. You need a detailed map to avoid getting lost.
- **Resource planning:** When you've established a credible close date, you can begin planning the post-sales activities of your professional services, account management, and support teams.

* GAME PREP *

So, you've just received an OK from the prospect confirming that they want to buy from you. You're feeling pretty good about your deal and life in general. This is the point at which it's easy to fall into the complacency trap and assume that the prospect—who just told you that he wants your product—will drop everything else and work tirelessly to complete this transaction. Rather than relaxing, you should actually be pushing even harder to complete the final steps in the buying process and get the contract signed. It's time to introduce the CP to the prospect, so start by calling your contact to let them know it's coming:

> *"Tim, I'm really excited to work with you on this important project. Could we find 15 to 20 minutes to discuss our next steps together? The goal would be to understand all remaining steps in your contracting process, identify who will be involved, and establish a timeline to meet your February 1 start date. I'll use this information to create a close plan for both of us to ensure that the process runs smoothly and the contract gets signed in January."*

In terms of formatting the CP, I prefer MS Word, Excel or PowerPoint, and recommend creating a "living" document that can be easily updated and shared. Email templates are more difficult to amend and easier to lose in a cluttered email inbox.

The letter format is what I use most frequently; here's a sample CP letter to get you started:

December 1, 2016

Mr. Timothy Shepherd, SVP Sales
ABC Corporation
1 ABC Way
Boston, MA 02111

Dear Tim,

I'm very pleased that you're interested in working with Savvy Sales to help you drive more inbound leads and improve lead response times at ABC Corp. You've indicated a desire to begin our work together on February 1, and we'll need a signed contract no later than December 28 to meet this start date. Per our conversation, we've identified the following actions, people, and dates as the remaining steps in our process:

1. Finance Committee Approval
    *   ABC Owner: Tim S. Due date: Dec 10.
2. Legal Review & Approval
    *   ABC Owners: Tim S. & Sue (counsel). Due date: Dec 15.
    *   Savvy Owners: Jonathan & Bill (counsel). Due date: Dec 18.
3. IT Security Signoff.
    *   ABC Owner: Barbara R. (CTO). Due date: Dec 21.
    *   Tim S. to research if John F. can also sign off on this.
4. Final Signatures
    *   Savvy: Jonathan J. Due date: Dec. 28
    *   ABC Owner: Tim S. Due date: Dec. 28.

As agreed, you and I will take responsibility for working with our respective teams to ensure that tasks are completed on schedule. I will distribute an updated plan each Friday detailing our progress. I'm looking forward to working with you and making ABC a successful Savvy customer. Thank you again for your business and support.

Best regards,
Jonathan

As you work from this template to create your own CP, make sure that you include the following elements:

- **Restatement of business goals:** This is a best practice in all of your correspondence with prospects, including the CP.
- **Tasks to be completed:** A detailed list of every single task that remains in the procurement process. Your contact knows their internal process much better than you do, so ask him/her to validate the task list.
- **Owner:** These are the people on both sides who'll work to complete each task and be held accountable.
- **Status indicator:** Tracks progress on each activity as open, closed, or in-process.
- **Due dates**: Every task must have a completion date. If you're meeting every deadline, your deal is on track. If dates are slipping, work with your sponsor to fix this; a pattern of missed dates can indicate trouble.
- **Sponsors:** The sponsors on both sides own the overall process and will be the first points of contact if you run into trouble.

I've helped a number of companies set up the CP in their CRM system as a template for reps to update. This approach brings discipline to the practice and makes the CP a required step in every deal. It also makes the close process transparent, so management can track updates and progress as your deal moves closer to signature.

* SHOWTIME *

Because the CP is essentially a guide through the prospect's procurement process, it's important that you always develop this document in collaboration with your contact. They know their process much better than you do, and their input is invaluable. Not only will they map out the remaining steps to produce a signed contract, they'll fill in the blanks with the names of people who will be critical for certain tasks—lawyers, security specialists, procurement contacts, and executives. As your sponsor is familiar with the company's buying process, he/she can give you a more accurate sense of how long each stage will take and the various personalities involved. Make sure that your sponsor signs off on the final version of the CP; their validation signals that they also want to sign the deal and are willing to commit the necessary time and resources.

Once you have a CP that both parties have agreed to, you need to don your project management hat and micro-manage the buying process to completion. It's OK if completion dates slip a bit—busy people have other priorities too—as long as it doesn't jeopardize the final close date. Stay vigilant and look for missed dates and other patterns that could indicate future trouble. When unforeseen bumps do occur, you can lean on your sponsor to push people who are missing their commitments. The CP should be updated as tasks are completed, and I either post this document to a shared drive or send an updated version to my counterpart at the end of each week.

CPs are also a winning strategy when you're offering time-based incentives. For example, I recently offered a client a 10% discount to sign our contract by December 31. Since the timeframe was ambitious and the team was new to buying software, I added the condition that the client needed to work with me to create a detailed CP. They agreed, and we both received an education on their complicated internal purchasing process. With every task, owner and date crisply defined in the CP, we were able to sign the contract a week ahead of schedule. I shudder to think what would've happened without the CP, because the complexity of their process was eye-opening on both sides. The CP became our insurance policy to navigate the process and sign the deal.

The CP doesn't guarantee a 100% close rate—nothing can—but it does give you the best possible chance of delivering your committed deals. Plus, you'll avoid nasty, last-minute surprises and hard conversation with your sales manager about the one that got away. The CP should be a mandatory step for every committed deal, and you'll see the difference it makes in your close process and your results.

#23: Make an Executive Play

Your sales career depends on your ability to connect and work with executives and decision-makers. By engaging with the leaders who make things happen, you can maneuver around endless sales cycles and indecisive project teams.

The Executive Play ("EP") is a high-risk, high-reward technique that involves both an enhanced degree of difficulty and greater potential for a big payoff. The essence of the EP is that you approach the decision-maker in your deal and ask them for a decision: to buy, to accelerate the sales cycle, or to increase their investment with you. The EP can be very useful when you're deal is stuck, or if you're working with low-level contacts who have trapped you in an endless evaluation cycle. In these cases, the executive can be pressed to commit more resources or make a buy decision. It's a pure power play on your part, and one that can save you from spinning your wheels with a recalcitrant prospect who's content to burn up your time without making a commitment.

When you initiate the EP, it can seal your current deal and present opportunities to address more strategic challenges in the business *if you're prepared.* **Never** approach an executive with a weak business case because it'll kill your current deal and probably any hopes of future business. Politics and personalities both play a large role in the EP, and it demands a high level of skill and finesse to execute well. For this reason, it's one of the more advanced techniques among *The 40 Best*, and more difficult to master if you're a newcomer to sales.

As we progress in our sales careers, there are many expectations that follow us. One of these is the belief that senior salespeople have developed the experience and gravitas to work with executives on the client side. This is commonly referred to as *executive selling*, and in many ways it's like traveling abroad. First-time travelers stumble and make mistakes, while experienced travelers speak the language, understand social norms, and feel more at ease. The more experience you gain with executive selling, the easier it will become.

Unfortunately, the executives themselves don't make it easy for you. They're busier than ever: it's estimated that executives spend 40 to 50 percent of their time—100 days per year—in meetings. They're protected by multiple gatekeepers specifically instructed to detect and deflect determined salespeople. Your ability to connect with the executive will ultimately depend on (1) a smart and persistent approach, (2) the right conditions for engagement, (3) establishing your credibility, and (4) communicating your message in terms that will resonate at their level.

Endless Evaluations, or Deal by Committee

In my experience, executives don't concern themselves with routine matters like product purchases. As much as we'd like to believe that we're important, executives are content to delegate this responsibility to a project team. "Deals by Committee" are the norm in sales today, and you can expect five or more critical stakeholders involved in every B2B purchasing decision. If these stakeholders are low-level people, or just disagree with each other, then you can get stuck on the corporate gerbil wheel—running furiously but never making any progress.

This scenario is ideal for the EP because you're presented with a stark choice: continuing to waste valuable time and resources with the committee, or go around them and approach the executive. For better or worse, you know that the executive can make *something* happen, and this is preferable to a lengthy, painful evaluation process. If you're skilled in your approach, you can force a decision and win the business. If you're clumsy, you'll offend the stakeholders and sabotage your deal. It's a balancing act that requires proficiency and skill, so let's explore how the executive play should (and shouldn't) be executed.

* GAME PREP *

Consider the executive mindset: how they think, what they value, and what gets their attention. Executives aren't worried about product features, but rather how you'll help them grow their business, improve efficiency and make more money. You need to think big-picture, and stay out of the technical weeds when discussing your product. *Always* bring new ideas to the table: executives are generally smart people who want to hear insightful opinions from other smart people. If you have experience in their industry, it's important to highlight this and build your credibility.

Relationships are very important at senior levels, and you want to develop a rapport with the executive before launching into your pitch. When I first started attending executive-level meetings with my CEO, I was confused by how long it took them to actually discuss business. They seemed to talk about everything *but* business. What I didn't realize was that the executives were sizing each other up and making spot decisions concerning trust, intelligence, and whether they saw this person as a partner. **The first five minutes are the most important in any executive meeting, and I've seen reps sabotage their chances by rushing the business conversation before it's time.** When an executive starts checking their phone, you know you're dead, and it's extremely hard to win the executive back once you've lost them.

The language you choose is important to communicate the right message at the right level. You want to elevate the conversation to address concepts that will resonate with the executive. Try these executive selling tips to improve your performance and outcomes:

- DO speak to the value of your solution by using terms like *ROI, measurable business improvement*, and *strategic goals*.
- DO be transparent and straightforward when conversing; most executives have finely-tuned B.S. detectors, and "sales-speak" will get you (politely) thrown out the door.
- DO teach them something about their business that they don't already know.
- DO come to the table with solutions and tangible next steps, but also consider this little trick when making your pitch to executives: rather than presenting a fully-formed idea, plant the seeds and let *them* come up with the answer on their

own. In this way, they'll feel a sense of ownership in the idea and support it.
- DON'T be too technical or focus on the minutiae of product features.
- DON'T be intimidated by titles. Executives are just like you and me, only with a bit more responsibility. They strive to do a good job, worry about meeting goals and want to impress their boss. Approach them with confidence and conviction, and you'll succeed.

Executives like to believe that they're decisive, and this is why the EP can give your deal the energy jolt it needs. Your goal is to get a decision and a commitment, and how skillfully you present your case is often the difference between success and failure. Selling at an executive level is not a destination but a journey, so expect to make some missteps along the way. Learn from these and keep at it; you'll improve with every engagement and gain confidence in your abilities.

* SHOWTIME *

Once you've decided to initiate the EP, consider the nature of your relationship with the executive. This will determine the extent of your challenge and the best course of action. Below are three common scenarios for the EP:

Best-case Scenario: You know the executive, and he/she is involved in your deal. You feel comfortable initiating a conversation with them.

If the executive has been hands-on in the sales process, chances are that you've built some level of rapport with them. In this case, they'll take your call, so it's completely appropriate for you to discuss the strategy of your deal. Even if it's a "deal by committee," the executive has significant input and veto authority on the decision.

Once you've begun dealing with the executive, make sure you're not pushed down to lower-level people. The evaluators and team members need your attention as well, of course, but once you and the executive start talking, you want to keep all conversations at this level. While deals with a hands-on executive tend to move at a faster pace, they can still become mired in indecision and overshadowed by other priorities. **An active relationship with the executive represents your best chance of making the EP work**. When you're ready, schedule time on the executive's calendar and make your pitch:

> *"Hello, Fiona, it's good to speak with you again. We've discussed how my solution will play an important part in your overall strategy to increase efficiencies by 50%, and I know this is an important area of focus for you. I know you have an ambitious timeline, and it seems as though we've recently lost some momentum. I wanted to share five reasons why my company would be the best partner for you, and with your agreement present a plan that would enable us to get started right away to meet your desired timeline."*

Be bold and don't be afraid to ASK the executive for a commitment. You've come this far, and now it's do-or-die time. If their answer is "Yes," you need to be prepared to implement a plan of action. If their answer is "No," at least you know where you stand and can decide whether or not to keep pursuing this business. If the answer is "Yes, but—" or they defer to the evaluation team, your follow-up question should be, *"What would it take to get your commitment to work with me?"* Usually, this question produces a list of outstanding issues that need to be addressed before you can sign the deal (see **#18: ASK for the Business**). Fix these issues and your deal's back on track with a clear line of sight to a signed contract. Ask the executive for their help removing any obstacles that might impede your progress, and get to work closing this client.

Most Common Scenario: You know who the executive is, but he/she isn't really involved in the deal. You may have met and spoken with him/her before, but there's no real relationship in place.

This happens all the time because executives usually don't bother themselves with the mechanics of a vendor selection process. You may have met them on the first call, but they've since delegated the work to their project team and rarely show up for meetings. When your access to the executive is limited, you have two choices: (1) work through your contacts to ask for a formal introduction, or (2) cold-call the executive.

Let's focus on soliciting an internal introduction, as this is your best option. You *never* want to convey the appearance of going over someone's head; this rarely goes well and is more apt to kill your opportunity than help it. I've seen reps make clumsy end-runs around their contact in an attempt to reach the executive, and before I could warn them, they lost the deal. People on the evaluation team may not be the final decision-makers, but they can make sure you're dropped from consideration if you make them mad. Think long and hard about going around your contact before taking this step.

A much better approach is to ask your contact to set up a call and make the introduction. **Asking for an executive introduction is a trial-close, because nobody is going to introduce a dead-end vendor to their boss.** When your contact agrees to connect you with their executive, it's a good sign for your deal. Try these approaches:

- Make an offer that the contact needs the executive to approve. Set up a call to walk them both through it.
- Adjust your value proposition to address more strategic imperatives that will resonate with the executive, and make sure they know about it.
- Introduce your own executive into the process (see **#6: New Faces**) and invite them to your next meeting. Request that your contact do the same.
- Simply ask your contact to make the introduction.

Before your meeting with the executive, research his/her background through LinkedIn and Google searches. If the executive recently gave a speech, watch it on video; this can be a great conversation-starter. Find topics that will help you to establish a good rapport before you talk business. Share an article that you have written, talk about your work with a competitor, or tell them something they don't know about their own business. This will build your credibility and get the conversation flowing.

Expect them to be direct and respond in kind. "I'd like to work with you, and I'm here to ask what it will take to win your business," is an effective opening, and often leads to a productive discussion. It's not often that you have an audience with the executive, so make the most of this opportunity to move your business forward. The good news is that this meeting gives you the OK to start working with the executive, so be sure to keep the lines of communication open and don't let yourself get pushed back down to the evaluation team.

What if you ask your contact to make an introduction and they decline? This puts you in the difficult position of having to weigh the implications of calling the executive against the certainty that this action will anger your contact. There is no right answer, and you need to read the situation and use your best judgment.

Worst-case Scenario: You have to cold-call the executive.

Successfully beginning a dialogue with an executive by cold-calling them is one of the most difficult challenges faced by a salesperson. Unfortunately, it happens more often than any of us would like, and the reality is that there are times when making a cold approach to the executive is your last and only option, such as:

- You're dealing with a hostile, biased, or lethargic evaluation team.
- Your contact refuses your request to introduce you to the executive.
- Your contact doesn't know the executive because they're much higher in the corporate hierarchy.
- For whatever reason, you've decided to throw caution to the wind and make a final "death or glory" plea for the business.

Obviously, each of these is a long shot, and your odds of succeeding are slim. That said, there are certain actions you can take to improve your chances. Let's consider your approach and how best to either work through the executive's EA or contact the executive directly.

The EA is the executive's first line of defense, and they're paid to thwart persistent salespeople. They always seem to pick up the phone when you call, and the executive is invariably traveling or tied up in a meeting. While pursuing a top executive at a large food company, I got to know his EA quite well, and she told me that she screens every call, email and voicemail before determining which of these make it through to the executive. *Think the executive is listening to your eloquent voicemail? Wrong—I guarantee their EA is listening to it first.* Working the EA requires patience and a certain amount of finesse, so try the following:

- Be polite and friendly. The EA often decides who makes it through to the executive, and he/she can make or break your effort. It helps your chances if they like you.
- Request ten minutes to make your pitch. Take any available timeslot you can get.
- Call the executive's office and explain why you're calling. Ask their EA if the executive handles this type of request. Most likely, the EA will point you to someone on the executive's staff (VP or Director). Ask the EA if he/she could forward your information and let this person know you'll be calling; you now have an internal referral from a well-placed contact. One EA specifically instructed the Director's EA to put me through to him when I called, and this approach worked beautifully.

If you attempt to bypass the EA and approach the executive directly, it's more difficult (but not impossible) to make this connection. Here are several tips to succeed with the (cold) executive approach:

- Find the executive on social media and send him/her a direct message. Most executives maintain these accounts themselves, so you don't have to worry about the EA intercepting your messages.

166

- Call early or late when the executive is working but the EA has gone home. If the executive answers the phone, remember that you have about 10 seconds to spark their interest. Practice your pitch until it's crisp and concise.
- Anticipate objections and/or the "brush off" by planning your responses beforehand.
- If you get voicemail, keep your message to 30 seconds (or less). Present two compelling reasons why the executive should call you back.
- Remember, language counts when addressing the executive. Emphasize strategic objectives that you know are important and quantify the business value that you'll deliver.
- Drop names whenever you can—colleagues, competitors, or even your day-to-day contact at their company. This introduces familiarity and establishes a purpose for your call.

PART FOUR

Play the Game

Sales *is* a game, and it's your job to excel at it. When you sharpen your skills, do more of the right things, and execute every day, you're playing the game at a high level. This is the key to winning and reaching your personal, financial, and career goals.

The techniques in **Play the Game** will help you to master the sales game: fill your pipeline, move prospects from maybe to yes, deliver a killer pitch, build relationships and trust, and prioritize your daily activities. Play the game well and you'll conquer the leaderboard, secure your spot at President's Club, and make more money.

The 7 techniques presented in **Play the Game** include:

#24: The Call Blitz
Sales is a numbers game; the more people you engage, the greater your chances of finding the buyers. **The Call Blitz** channels your prospecting efforts into a concerted, highly-focused calling campaign that will fill your pipeline in one day.

#25: Party Like It's 1999
Everyone likes a party, and events are opportunities to network with your target audience and build the personal relationships that lead to better business relationships.

#26: Calling All Competition
Everyone is interested in what the competition is up to. Competitors will move quickly and decisively to close gaps when they think they're falling behind. Call every one of your customer's competitors and sell them the same value proposition that worked for your customer.

#27: Prospect Your A** Off

There's a proven formula to *owning* the leaderboard: (1) target the right companies; (2) get on the phone; and (3) start prospecting your ass off. There's really no substitute for smart, steady prospecting in sales.

#28: Raise the Curtain on Act II

F. Scott Fitzgerald once said, "There are no second acts in American lives." There are, however, second *chances* with your prospects. If people didn't buy the first time around, call them again and set the stage for a sale.

#29: Hit the Road Jack

There's no substitute for a face-to-face meeting in sales. Hit the road and meet with your best customers and prospects.

#30: Eat Your Way to Success

Food is a common bond that brings people together. Dine out often with your clients, and use this opportunity to build strong relationships that lead to sales.

#24: The Call Blitz

Sales is a numbers game; the more people you engage, the greater your chances of finding the buyers. **The Call Blitz** *channels your prospecting efforts into a concerted, highly-focused calling campaign that will fill your pipeline in one day.*

I've been a part of many sales organizations in which the concept of the "call blitz" was a sacred part of the sales culture. The concept of the blitz is one full day devoted solely to outbound calling and initiating new conversations with prospects. It's the day you turn off your email and pick up the phone, because the name of the game is pipeline generation. I've seen reps generate $300K in qualified pipeline in a single day of blitzing, and this type of result isn't unusual. All it takes is a good call list, focus, and a commitment to pound the phones until you've reached your goals.

When I was selling for Oracle, call blitzes were a mandatory weekly activity for everyone in Oracle Direct, the company's inside sales organization. Imagine thousands of sales reps each making 80 to 100 calls in a single day, and you can begin to picture the tsunami of pipeline that this activity would generate for Oracle *every week*.

Each blitz would focus on a new product and include a one-hour training session to communicate product details and familiarize everyone with the pitch. On blitz day, there was a level of intensity and competition that pushed everyone to make more calls, initiate more conversations and generate more pipeline. It was not uncommon for reps to exceed 100 calls on blitz day and produce hundreds of thousands of dollars in new pipeline. Results were closely tracked and awards presented to the top performers. The weekly call blitz was ingrained in the Oracle culture, and it became a primary source of nourishment for the company's sales pipeline.

The blitz concept is specifically designed to maximize the two variables that every salesperson has complete control over: where they spend their time and how hard they work. Call blitzes challenge you to push yourself on the prospecting front and maintain intense focus on a single activity—outbound calling—for an entire day. I'll be the first to admit that it can be difficult to maintain focus and enthusiasm for eight hours; picking up the phone and calling 75 to 100 people is mentally and physically exhausting. When you see the results, however, you'll become a believer.

The reality is that prospecting is often the first activity that sales reps cut out of their schedules when they get busy. Nobody really likes to prospect anyway, so it's easy to skip it and hope that somehow your pipeline will build itself. On the other hand, the reps who climb the leaderboard and earn President's Club honors understand the importance of prospecting, and this one-day burst of calling can be more productive than a week of half-hearted prospecting. The call blitz requires discipline and commitment, but once you see its power and impact on your business, it'll become a staple in your arsenal of sales weapons.

* GAME PREP *

Good blitz preparation consists of creating a high-value list of prospects, perfecting your message, clearing your calendar, minimizing distractions, and adopting the right mental attitude to sustain a day of intense calling.

We've discussed how much easier it is to sell to customers than brand-new prospects. For this reason, call blitzes targeting the customer base can generate tangible results quickly, and upselling the customer base is often a good place to start. Blitzes are also employed to attract new logos, and you'll need to work with Marketing or mine your CRM to create a call list of 125 to 150 prospect names. Validate that every contact has a phone number, because you don't want to waste time looking these up on blitz day. If your list is digital, print a hard copy; computers always seem to freeze or crash at the most inopportune times, and you don't want to be stuck in neutral on blitz day.

Choosing the right product or theme for your blitz is important. My company once ran a blitz promoting one of our more technical products, and the results were terrible. It just took too long to explain the product to prospects. Simplicity is key; I never choose more than one theme or product for a blitz, and the message needs to be straightforward and simple. When the goal is call volume, a solution that requires ten minutes of explanation won't cut it. Instead, choose a product with a shorter sales cycle and a pitch that's easy for the prospect to understand. Consider the "WOW" factor, because you want a message that will immediately capture the prospect's attention. Sizzle sells, and products that sizzle are more likely to lead to good conversations and new pipeline.

Write a script that distills the blitz topic down to one or two key points. A pre-written script helps you move with greater speed and confidence, and can also be converted easily into an email template. An approach I've seen work well is to email your message to everyone on your blitz list a week in advance. When you call these people on blitz day, they've already read your email and recognize your name, and this approach can improve your connection and conversion rates.

As you prepare your messaging, educate yourself on product features and make sure you can deliver both a high-level pitch and answers to more detailed questions as they come up. Storytelling works, so memorize relevant customer stories that will bring more color to your pitch. Optimally, you also have a brief marketing PDF that you can attach to your follow-up email. The use of incentives can create an important Call-to-Action on blitz day, so consider offering special terms as part of your campaigns.

Timing the blitz is important; mid-week works better than Mondays or Fridays, which can be travel days for the businesspeople you want to catch at their desks. When you pick your blitz date, block out the entire day on your calendar. Let your colleagues know that you're committed for the day and won't be accepting other meetings. Focus is critical on blitz day, and distractions need to be minimized. You know what distracts you during the day, so close the door, shut down email, and direct your focus towards calling and pitching your list of prospects.

* SHOWTIME *

When blitz day arrives, first check the small things that are easy to overlook. Make sure that your phone is charged and in good working order. You want to keep hydrated, so have plenty of water on hand. Caffeine is OK to start your engines, but it can be hard on your voice during an intense day of calling. Skip that second cup of joe and drink water or tea instead. Closing your office door will minimize the sounds and distractions of a busy workplace. I remember one rep who hung a "Salesperson at work – Do Not Disturb" sign on his office door, a humorous but firm warning to colleagues to leave him alone. Close your email (you can check it on breaks) and Web browser to minimize the temptation to read emails or surf the 'Net.

Set specific and measurable goals for yourself by thinking about what you want to achieve and the outcomes you're looking to drive. As the day unfolds, give yourself time to assess your progress against these goals and make adjustments where needed. To keep myself focused, I often write my goals in big block letters on the whiteboard in my office:

> *I **will** make 100 calls today, have 10 substantial conversations, book two meetings with prospects and generate $100,000 in pipeline.*

Time management is important on blitz days. To benchmark yourself, assume that each call will average three minutes. If your goal is 100 calls, that's 300 minutes or 5 hours of phone time. In a typical 8-hour day, your pace will be 12-14 calls per hour. Monitor your progress and take breaks to stretch and clear your head. Before you return to the phone, take a few minutes to assess how you're doing. Are you on pace to meet your goals? Is your pitch resonating? Are prospects engaging with you and asking questions? It's important to be flexible and make adjustments to drive the best possible outcome.

My call script is the variable that I change most often, and I've found it useful to start my blitz day with two or three different scripts. I'll spend an hour pitching one script, then switch to another and compare results. Writing a good script is critical and can make the difference between a great day and an average day. If you can't settle on the right messaging, postpone the blitz until you feel prepared. **Don't waste a good prospecting list pitching a message that isn't working.**

While you may let the call flow develop naturally, remember to steer conversations towards your desired objective. **Your objective should be a commitment from the prospect: to buy; review your information; invite their colleagues to a demonstration; or simply talk again later. Don't hang up until you've accomplished your goal.** If the conversation wanders, gently steer the prospect back to the topic at hand. Keep the prospect talking and learn whatever you can to help you in the sales process. Don't rush prospects just to hit high call-volume targets; substantive conversations with likely buyers are much more important than simply making a lot of calls.

The Oracle commitment to call blitzes is a testament to their power and effectiveness, and Oracle reps blitzed four times a month, twelve months a year. Over time, the entire salesforce became expert call blitzers, and results reflected this greater proficiency. Take a page from one of the biggest and most successful sales organizations in the world and make call blitzes a standard technique in your sales arsenal.

#25: Party Like It's 1999

Everyone likes a party, and events are opportunities to network with your target audience and build the personal relationships that lead to better business relationships.

My wife and I recently received an invitation to a seminar exploring the wonderful world of Florida condominium timeshares. In exchange for our attendance, we'd receive a free flatscreen TV. We checked our schedules, decided that a free TV was worth three hours of our time and accepted the invitation. Additionally, because I'm in sales, I figured this event would be market research to provide a glimpse into a sales process that is totally different from my own experience.

The seminar, held at a Boston hotel, reminded me of a revival meeting, with customer testimonials and tightly-edited videos of gorgeous houses and people living "the Florida lifestyle." Brilliant pink plastic flamingoes ringed the meeting room, and each of us was draped with a Hawaiian lei as we entered (even though these had nothing to do with Florida). It all looked pretty nice, and the fact that it was January in Boston certainly added to the allure. The pitch itself was constant and steady, culminating with a special offer to seal the deal: *sign up today and you'll receive an additional week at no charge.*

It was a pretty compelling offer until I read the fine print and learned that the free week was in August, which seemed a less than perfect time to visit Florida. When the seminar concluded, the event team swarmed the room armed with clipboards, with the singular purpose of signing-up people on the spot. After spending three hours together with several other couples, there was definitely pressure to sign a contract, and nobody (including us) wanted to be the ones who ruined the party and said "No."

As we were really there for the free TV, we did decline, and quickly left once we claimed our prize. In retrospect, I have to give kudos to the sales team because they hit on all the right elements for a successful event: invite a pre-screened audience; create a fun and electric atmosphere (to mask the hard sell); serve good food; create a compelling offer; and apply pressure in all the right places. I'm sure the formula works for them more often than not. While B2C sellers have leveraged the power of the sales event for years, it remains an underutilized channel in the B2B world.

Everybody likes a party. Events are powerful because they provide a different venue for the same core message: *buy my products*. Professionals like to network with their peers, listen to dynamic speakers, and eat free food. In a less formal atmosphere, people lower their defenses and interact on a more personal level. You can really get to know your buyers, and step outside of your sales persona to give people a glimpse of the real you. Whether it's a new product launch or cocktail hour for networking events provide an opportunity to shift the conversation from the boardroom to the ballroom and strip away the formality of the buyer-seller interaction. By designing the right kind of events that will appeal to your buyers, you'll have an opportunity to pitch your products, show off your thought leadership, connect with people on a whole new level, and ultimately drive your sales agenda in the right direction.

* GAME PREP *

Events cost money, so your first step is to speak to your manager about available budget to fund your event. In my experience, Sales & Marketing often have discretionary budget set aside for events, so make sure you ask. The type of event you're planning will determine who you invite, but generally it's going to be your top prospects and customers. In terms of balance, try to invite one customer for every three prospects. Customers are your biggest supporters, and their endorsement carries weight. Seeding your event with friendly customers gives you an extended sales team to deliver your message, so make the effort to introduce your customers and prospects and then stand back and let them talk. Your customer will do the selling for you.

The outcome you're trying to achieve often determines the nature of your event. New-product launches that push a customer to buy right away are structured differently than networking events or seminars designed to educate and inform. Here's a list of event formats to consider for your next killer sales event:

- **New-product launches:** Your clients are always interested in new products. Watch Steve Jobs launch the iPod and the iPhone to see just how powerful these events can be.
- **Executive networking:** These gatherings work especially well if you can deliver A-list attendees. It's not often that busy executives get to rub shoulders with their peers, and this will drive their attendance. Executives need a month to clear their calendars, and phone calls to lobby for attendance can ensure a good turnout. Prominent speakers can become a draw at these events, so call in some favors to book a heavyweight.
- **Conference/tradeshow events:** Take advantage of opportunities to piggyback on already-established events that your targeted audience will be attending. Host a dinner, sponsor a happy hour, or invite people to a local sporting event.
- **Regional roundtables:** Moderate a roundtable discussion on important topics and include plenty of time for networking.
- **Customer appreciation:** It never hurts to thank the people who keep the lights on. Don't worry; you can upsell them on new products and upgrades while thanking them for their support.
- **Holiday parties:** Throw a holiday party and invite *everyone*!
- **Sporting events:** Everybody likes to attend a live game. Buy tickets and invite a few individuals, or rent a corporate box (if budget allows).
- **Lunch or Dinner:** Your sales event can be as simple as a formal dinner. I've probably finalized more deals in restaurants than I have in the office.

Your marquee is the headline that will attract people to your event. Work with Marketing and PR to create an attention-grabbing marquee that will compel people to sign up for your event. Here are three marquee concepts that have worked for me:

- **Guest speakers:** The more well-known and respected your speaker is, the better your draw will be. Beware of paying high speaker fees that cut into your margins. In many cases, you can find the perfect speaker through your extended network and not pay a dime.
- **Special offers and incentives:** Offer every attendee a light version of your product, or allow them to use it free-of-charge for a month. You *will* convert 25-30% of these prospects into customers.
- **Drawings or giveaways:** 3D printers and drones have replaced iPads as the hot giveaway items. Give attendees the chance to win something cool and they'll show up at your event.

Question: What's the difference between an optional meeting and a mandatory meeting?
Answer: Free pizza.

Allocate part of your event budget for food. People expect to be fed at events, and you don't want hungry attendees excusing themselves early and skipping your presentation. The food selection doesn't have to be sumptuous, but you do need to provide something. If you have the budget, pay for an hour of free cocktails—it will loosen people up and give them a reason to stay.

If you're making a presentation, make sure that your content is crisp, relevant and fresh. You don't want attendees nodding off. Guest speakers are better than droning monologues; interactive sessions are better than death by PowerPoint. Setting aside time for networking is key, and the more opportunities you give people to connect, the better. This goes twice as much for salespeople, who should be working the room, shaking hands, and having the types of conversations that lead to future sales.

* SHOWTIME *

On the day of your event, show up early and make sure the venue is in order, the collateral is laid out, the coffee is hot, etc. If you have a team working together, brief every member on their responsibilities beforehand and oversee their efforts. **Everyone is a salesperson at a sales event**, so encourage your team members to circulate and meet as many attendees as possible. It's all about networking, connecting with people, and laying the groundwork for future business.

Don't be shy about selling yourself at the event. The attendees know what to expect, and you have every right to pitch your products and ASK for people's business. It may be a hard or soft sell depending upon the nature of the event, but you need to take advantage of a captive audience while you've got them. Hard sell events are a constant pitch—similar to my timeshare experience—while networking and dinner events are more low-key and focused on relationship-building. In many ways, the soft pitch can make a business conversation easier because people let their guards down. Everyone should depart feeling as though their time was well-spent, and this bodes well for attendance at your next event.

Inviting trusted customers to your events as "objective" third parties is a fantastic technique that always works. Your customers are living endorsements for your products, and a good word from them gives you instant credibility. Make a point to introduce your best customers to your most promising prospects, then step back and let your customer do the selling for you. The business-card drop is another winning technique, especially if you're giving away a free gift like a 3D printer or drone that gets people's attention. If you're holding a drawing to select the winner, it can't hurt to pick one of your top prospects, and delivering the good news to them inevitably leads to a business conversation.

A salesperson I admire once told me that her goal with any event is to create a shared experience with her client. It could be a random restaurant that turns out to be amazing, a fantastic bottle of wine or a rude waiter. It's a memory that you and your client can recall with fondness, almost like an inside joke. **These shared experiences build relationships, and relationships lead to sales. People buy from people they like.** Events are perfect opportunities to break out of your sales role, get to know your clients on a more personal level. When you can enjoy yourself *and* forward your business agenda, it's always a winning combination.

#26: Calling All Competition

Everyone is interested in what the competition is up to. Competitors will move quickly and decisively to close gaps when they think they're falling behind. Call every one of your customer's competitors and sell them the same value proposition that worked for your customer.

One of the central messages of this book is the importance of the prospects and customers already in your pipeline if your goal is generating revenue as quickly as possible. The logic is straightforward: a company that's not on your radar today won't be buying from you in three months; corporate American just doesn't work that fast. Hoping for one of these "bluebirds" to fly through your window and save your quarter is a pipe dream, not a strategy. There *are* exceptions, however and one of these is the buyer driven by competitive pressures. These companies will move rapidly through the sales cycle when they're feeling the heat of competitive pressure and believe that they're falling behind.

Short of a personal referral, the quickest way to begin a discussion with a prospect is to mention the fact that you're doing business with their competitor. Technology has supercharged business like never before, contributing to the underlying buzz of paranoia evident in corporate boardrooms everywhere. It's a nagging belief that someone, somewhere, is working on something that will redefine the market, steal my customers and make my business obsolete. And guess what? Sheer size alone won't protect you; in fact it's a detriment. Many of my Fortune 100 clients are terrified that they won't see the threat coming until it's too late. Their solution is to spend their way out of trouble. They'll seize on any morsel of competitive intelligence they can find, and if the solution means throwing money at the same products their competitors are using, so be it. This is your opportunity.

Before you pursue this strategy, remember that while dropping your client's name will open the door, you *cannot* under any circumstances reveal confidential information about your clients that's not already in the public domain. It's a bit of a tease on your part; **you want to dangle the promise of inside information without actually revealing any inside information**. The prospect doesn't know this of course, and sometimes they'll take your call just to see what you're willing to share. Once this door is open, it's up to you to walk on through and turn this prospect into a customer.

* GAME PREP *

Begin by reviewing your current portfolio of customers. Look for market leaders first, because these are the companies that everyone else benchmarks against. For example, you'll have instant credibility with competing oil and gas companies when you tell them that Exxon is one of your customers. If you have an Exxon case study, send it to these companies and follow up with a phone call. Case studies that contain ROI figures are even better, as they quantify how you can help oil and gas companies to achieve even greater success.

A strong success story with a company that your target prospect respects *will* open doors for you, especially if the prospect believes you can replicate these results for *them*. To build a call list, I'd focus on your customer's five biggest competitors. Validate these companies against your ICP, and don't waste your time calling prospects that don't fit your model. If you have a vertical focus, take the time to research market trends and customize your pitch. Look for articles, news, and press releases covering topics relevant to your message, and reference these in your communications. **Rather than casting a wide net, you're approaching highly-targeted prospects with a powerful message and the credentials to back it up. This is why these prospects will call you back.**

Let me share a personal story that reinforces the importance of research before calling a client. While selling innovation management software, I read an article about a speech by a CEO in which he made a bold commitment to—you guessed it—innovation. The CEO's company just happened to be a competitor of one of my most prominent customers. I called the CEO's office, explained to his EA why I was calling, and asked if the CEO handled this kind of request himself. He didn't, but she directed me to an SVP and instructed *his* office to put me through to the SVP when I called.

When I called the SVP, we discussed his CEO's innovation vision, and I related some of the work we were doing with their competitor. Since the CEO wanted to be seen as a leader—not a follower—in the innovation space, the revelation that they were already behind got everyone's attention. In the flurry of activity that followed, one of their actions was to muscle through a contract for my software platform. Bingo! In this case, good research, a targeted pitch, and the heat of competitive pressure drove the company to action, and I made my sale. Fear works in sales, and this is why **Calling All Competition** is included as one of *The 40 Best*.

Similar to **#14: Open Your Customer's Little Black Book**, your best tactic is to use your customer's name to get the prospect's attention. Make it prominent in all of your messaging. Since calling your customer's competitor is essentially a cold call, referencing your customer will help you to rise above the noise and deliver a commanding message: *your competition is doing something that you're not. This should interest you.* Here are some tricks to create a compelling message and get yourself noticed:

- Use a brief "teaser" about your work with the customer and insinuate that you're willing to share more. *"Company A is using our products to drive 20% growth across the board. I'd like to share more about what we're doing and discuss how we might achieve similar results for you."*
- Offer half of your message as a clue, and tell them they need to call you for the other half. *"I'm not sure if you know how Company A was able to drive 20% new growth last year, but better project execution was a big part of it. My company helped them to do this, and I'd like to share some ideas about how we could do the same for you."*
- Share ROI data from your case studies. Everyone likes to see real examples and real numbers.
- Drop names of people and companies.

- Demonstrate your knowledge of their market by providing insights that show off your thought leadership.
- Share lessons learned about challenges in their industry.

I've had more success with name-dropping than any other approach. People are more inclined to call you back when you've worked with a company or individual they know and respect. Rising above the noise to get the prospect's attention is the goal, and you'll know when a name resonate because *it's the first thing the prospect will ask you about when you connect.* Once your customer's name has opened the door, it's your job to walk on through and transform this prospect into a customer.

* SHOWTIME *

Calling All Competition is a targeted, outbound, lead-generation campaign that's less about lead quantity than *filling your pipeline with qualified prospects meeting your ICP and motivated by competitive pressures.* Since they compete with your customer, you know that your value proposition will resonate, and the competitive threat accelerates timelines and gives companies a reason to buy *now.* In my experience, some people will take the call just to see if you'll leak any tidbits of information about your customers. Once the door is open, qualify each prospect hard to verify available budget and urgency; you should know after the first call whether there's real potential for future business or if a prospect's just fishing for more information.

Below is a template for a "competitor" campaign that I sent out through email and LinkedIn InMail. Generally, my e-messages are brief and to-the-point, but I've extended the version below to illustrate several important points:

"Subject: How our work with P&G could help J&J

Dear J&J Executive:

I'm reaching out to introduce myself to see if we might set up 15 minutes for an introduction. My company does extensive work in the CPG space with companies like Procter & Gamble and Gillette, and we've developed unique insights and innovative branding techniques that I know would interest you.

We worked with Jess Smith at P&G to develop their "Brush Hard" campaign, which resulted in a 60% increase in sales. I believe there's a relevant use case for J&J in your current efforts to expand your dental-care business.

What we've learned through this work is that consumers are responding to "flash marketing" through wearable devices. Below is a link to an article describing our success with P&G, as well as a related case study for Gillette. I'll call your office next week to inquire about scheduling a call, and look forward to connecting."

Through this email, I've given the prospect a million reasons to call me back and learn more. I've established my credibility by referencing companies and people they know, and demonstrated that I have a successful track record generating results. This same template can also be leveraged to write a voicemail script. Use the 20-second rule (voicemail should be 20 seconds or less) to make sure your message is crisp and on-point:

"Hello, I'm calling because my company is quite active in the product-branding space. I currently work with P&G and Gillette, and through this work we've developed a number of insights that I know you'll find interesting. I'd like to request 15 minutes to share more about the great work we're doing with these clients, and how it could help you.

These days, everyone is worried about the competition. This is why **Calling All Competition** works. It's an opportunity to leverage your customer wins to sign their competition and dominate the market. Once you're established as the pre-eminent solution provider, your phone will start ringing as smaller players scramble to play catch-up. Use your customers as bait to go fishing for the competition, and you'll find that they *will* bite.

#27: Prospect Your A** Off

There's a proven formula to owning the leaderboard: (1) target the right companies; (2) get on the phone; and (3) start prospecting your ass off. There's really no substitute for smart, steady prospecting in sales.

Let's be honest; hardly anyone likes prospecting for new business. It's time-consuming, often boring, and generates lots of angst while providing little short-term reward. You open yourself up to indifference (at best) and sheer rudeness (at worst) because many businesspeople still believe it's acceptable to treat salespeople with disrespect. By the numbers, you'll have roughly 25 doors slammed in your face before one prospect finally invites you in. This ratio can be discouraging, and is the primary reason that most salespeople would rather eat broken glass (!) than pick up the phone and prospect.

Here's the truth: constant prospecting is the heartbeat of a successful sales effort. It's one of the key factors that distinguishes top performers from everyone else. Top sales leaders prospect every day; they make more phone calls, send more emails, connect with more people on social media and attend more networking events than everyone else. They don't believe Marketing and Inside Sales owe them a living, but instead take the initiative to create opportunities for themselves. They know that **the key to sales success is a full sales pipeline that is continuously being replenished with new opportunities, and that this responsibility ultimately lies with them.**

There are many reasons why salespeople fail, but two stand out:

1. they can't close, or
2. they don't have enough pipeline to meet their quota.

I can teach anyone to close, but building a sales pipeline is just back-breaking, mind-bending, soul-wrenching hard work. It's the price you pay for those big commission checks. There's no substitute, and no shortcut. The sooner you realize this and commit yourself to a program of disciplined, intelligent prospecting, the better your chances of climbing the leaderboard and making more money.

* GAME PREP *

My definition of prospecting is the act of conversing with an individual who meets your ICP criteria and could reasonably be expected to buy from you. Prospecting takes many forms, and these include personal meetings, phone conversations, email, social media, conferences, networking, referrals and follow-up on inbound leads. Unless prospects are knocking down the door to buy your products (we should all be so lucky), you'll want to incorporate all of these channels into a well-balanced prospecting effort.

None of this is new information, and every sales professional will acknowledge the importance of prospecting. Yet if this is the case, why do so many salespeople continue to make excuses? *I have other work to do; I'll prospect tomorrow; cold-calling doesn't work; why should I prospect when Marketing sends me leads; prospecting is for the new people; I'm too senior; I need to work my deals.*

In the spirit of full disclosure, I've made many of these excuses myself. Conducting an honest self-assessment about your level of commitment and attitude toward prospecting is a good first step. If you're putting in the work, terrific—you're likely seeing good results already. But if you're procrastinating and making excuses, you need an attitude adjustment. NOBODY makes it to the top of the leaderboard without a smart and steady prospecting effort.

Start by creating a prospecting plan for yourself that lists all of the specific tasks and actions you'll need to take. Your plan should include the following:

- **WHO** you're going to contact
- **HOW** you're going to reach them

- **WHEN** this activity will take place
- **WHAT** outcome you're trying to drive and how you'll measure your progress

WHO will be a combination of existing customers, prospects, new leads, and targeted cold calls. There's a definite hierarchy when it comes to prospecting. Your universe of sales contacts is like a pyramid: the apex represents your most important clients (to be called first), and you work your way down from there. Here's how I define my own prospecting pyramid, from the apex to the base:

- *Most Important*: Customers I'm trying to upsell; "hot" leads; current opportunities; referrals.
- *Important*: Qualified prospects that meet my ICP but lack budget or urgency; nurtured leads; tradeshow leads; former customers.
- *Low Priority*: Cold calls; companies using a competing product; leads older than one year.

Nearness to cash is a good reality check when prioritizing your prospecting activities. Anyone with a high probability of spending money with you in the next 3 to 6 months comes first, since they're the most likely to produce revenue for you in a short timeframe. As you work your way down the pyramid, the prospects are further from cash, and therefore a lower priority. The concept of nearness to cash should resonate with every salesperson and help you prioritize your call list.

HOW is your preferred communication channel: phone, email, snail mail, text, and social media. Actual conversations are the best in my opinion, so most of my prospecting time is spent dialing. **That said, it's important to note that certain channels work better to reach certain people**. If you know that your prospect answers her cell phone but never responds to emails, make sure you call her cell. *Even better, ASK the prospect how you should contact them*. They'll tell you exactly how to reach out in the future and get their attention.

WHEN is easy: block out 1-hour increments devoted solely to prospecting, and discipline yourself to keep this commitment. I recommend calling during peak selling hours (between 10am and 4pm) when people are at their desks. Minimize distractions and measure your progress; busy outbound reps can make up to 25 calls an hour. Once you develop a daily prospecting rhythm, you'll improve and find it less intimidating. Prospecting is not a one-time activity, but a daily commitment that gets easier when you discipline yourself to do it.

WHAT is the outcome you're looking to achieve on each call. Visualize the outcome before you dial; your goal might be closing a sale, gathering information, or setting the next appointment. When you know your desired outcome, you can guide the conversation in the right direction and do quick spot-checks to qualify the prospect.

* SHOWTIME *

The key to successful prospecting is discipline, repetition and planning. By adhering to these principles and putting some good, old-fashioned work behind it, I have no doubt you'll see results. Below are some best practices that will make the most of your prospecting time and help you maximize results. For more best practices around prospecting, also see **#24: The Call Blitz**:

Time blocking

Most salespeople can maximize their productivity and focus by prospecting in **1-hour blocks of time**. Prospecting is exhausting, and this is the perfect amount of time to maintain focus and keep your energy level high. Block off 1-hour increments during peak selling hours, and try to prospect for at least one hour every day. When you call during peak hours, you're more likely to catch people at their desks and actually have a conversation. Stick to calling, and defer low-yield activities like composing emails and posting to social media until the day is done.

Minimize distractions

Maintaining your focus is the key to improving productivity when it comes to prospecting. If you're being interrupted by your cell phone, incoming emails, notification messages, and co-workers banging on the door, your productivity is seriously compromised. The solution is simple: shut off email and social media and hang a "BUSY" sign on your door. You know what distracts you during the day, so make a point to eliminate these distractions before your start calling.

Avoid multitasking

Studies have shown that human beings perform much better when focused on a single task. Multitasking has become the bane of the modern professional, with literally dozens of channels competing for our attention every day. **We may *think* we're skilled multitaskers, but in reality most of us are just being mediocre at several things simultaneously**. Stay focused on the task at hand and avoid multitasking.

Know your outcome

Before I pick up the phone, I take a minute to brush up on each prospect's history and decide what I want to accomplish on the call. Whether I'm trying to get more information, drive action or stimulate interest in my product, I know the outcome I want to achieve. Once the call ends, I ask myself if I've met my objective. When you're consistently meeting your prospecting objectives, you're well on your way to becoming a star performer.

Defer administrative tasks

I'm a repeat offender when it comes to violating this rule, mainly because it's easy to get carried away after a good call and want to complete the follow-up actions immediately. But your prospecting time should be exactly that—time for prospecting. Administrative tasks like follow-up emails and creating new opportunities in your CRM are better handled after 5pm. Make a note of outstanding actions to be performed later, then keep your momentum going by making *another* good prospecting call.

#28: Raise the Curtain on Act II

F. Scott Fitzgerald once said, "There are no second acts in American lives." There are, however, second chances with your prospects. If people didn't buy the first time around, call them again and set the stage for a sale.

"You got the prospects coming in. You think they came in to get out of the rain? The guy don't walk on the lot unless he wants to buy. They're sitting out there waiting to give you their money. Are you gonna take it?"
- Alec Baldwin as "Blake" in *Glengarry Glen Ross*

Question: What's the difference between the prospects in your database and the rest of the world?
Answer: Your prospects told you that they want to buy.

Let's do a quick calculation: Estimate how many prospective customers you talked to in the past year. Now subtract the number of companies that actually bought from you. **What remains is a big list of qualified prospects that you need to call again.** Wherever you saw a spark of interest, it's incumbent on you to give these people and companies another chance to buy from you.

There are many reasons why prospects don't transform into customers: lack of budget or sponsorship; your product didn't meet their needs; they never called you back; the list goes on and on. If you consider every reason why prospects failed to buy from you, the common thread running through all of them is likely to be *bad timing*. The budget cycle was all wrong. The contact was traveling or absorbed with another project and never returned your calls. The company reorganized and everything changed.

Bad timing kills more potential deals than any other single factor. The good news, however, is that circumstances change, and yesterday's bad timing could be today's opportunity. You'll never know if you toss your old leads into the trashcan and forget about them, and this is why smart reps leverage a "nurture" list of past leads and run call campaigns that build upon that initial spark of interest.

As you look back on your leads from the past year, you'll find everything from companies you invested serious time to close, to people who never called you back. *They're not interested,* you think as you write them off your list and move on to the next name. I can't blame you; sales is a numbers game, and we must place our bets on the prospects that we believe will generate a big payoff.

On the other hand, it's that initial display of interest that separates our prospects from every other person in the world. At one point, they were engaged enough to call you or fill out a form on your website. If your timing is better now, this little spark might just lead to a sale. Before embarking on another disappointing cold-calling campaign, revive the people in your prospect list and reach out to them again. You may be surprised by their response the second time around.

* GAME PREP *

Most prospects are captured as leads within your CRM system, so start here to create your call list. For most sales organizations, there are easily a hundred names on this list if not more. Start with leads in the current year, and go back as far as fifteen months if needed to create a robust campaign. Optimally, you've recorded the reasons why the prospect failed to previously convert in your CRM system, and you can start making decisions about who to call.

I recommend being *inclusive* rather than *exclusive*, meaning that you should look for reasons to keep people on your call list. Here's why: I dug up an old lead from my *Lost* folder who had bought from a competitor. When I reached him on the phone, his first words were, "I'm so glad you called. Our implementation has been a disaster, and now the vendor wants to charge us more money. We made a mistake, and I need help." Although I initially had written off this company as a loss, circumstances changed, and I hit them at exactly the right time. It taught me a valuable lesson; **never write anybody off, and always keep in touch.**

Prospects who previously expressed strong interest and moved forward in the sales cycle are my first priority. To get their attention, I approach them with something new that will open the door to a conversation. Nobody responds well to the uninspired "*HiJimhowareyoudoingareyoureadytobuynow?*" message. **Every communication with a prospect – whether through phone or email – needs to stand on its own as valuable**. New white papers, thought-leadership pieces, articles and press releases give you a reason to get back in touch and see if timing and circumstances have changed. If you don't have any new content, take a page from **#3: Three New Ideas** and approach them with a couple of new ideas about how you can help them to grow and make more money, or develop your own content #**12: Develop a Content Strategy***)*.

An idea to get you started: mail a new white paper or marketing brief along with a handwritten personal note to your previous prospects. In the age of digital communication, a letter has a certain touch of elegance that will get you noticed. Send 5 to 10 letters every week, then follow up the next week with a call. Over a month, that's 25 to 40 solid conversations you can initiate with qualified prospects, and *this is kind of activity and volume that leads to financial results.*

* SHOWTIME *

Pick up the phone and start calling. I mean that. *Pick. Up. The. Phone.* Email is the calling card of a lazy salesperson. Actually speaking to the prospect enables you to dig deeper, ask questions and shape the dynamics of a conversation. You can learn more on a five-minute call than ten back-and-forth emails, so call everyone on your list.

My first question is to ask the prospect whether they've solved the business problem that brought them to me in the first place. Their answer tells me immediately whether I have an opportunity or not. If they've solved the problem or circumstances haven't changed in your favor, toss them back to Marketing for periodic email blasts and move on. If the need is still present and the conditions are right, you have a valid opportunity that can move faster than others because *the prospect already knows you and how your products could for their needs.* You may have previously spent weeks or months with the prospect trying to sell them, and this work didn't go to waste. This is how you **Raise the Curtain on Act II**, and your task now is to write a happier ending.

Be wary of the perpetual tire-kickers (also known as beautiful losers), who'll take you up (once again) on your offer to engage even though they have no intention of buying. They wasted your time before, and they'll do it again if you're not careful. **Qualify them hard with trial closes** by requesting an introduction to the executive, proposing an onsite meeting with the stakeholders, or requesting that the Legal team begin reviewing your contract. Asking for Legal's involvement is highly effective because **nobody pulls in the lawyers unless they're serious**. While your list of past prospects holds hidden promise, it's important to remember your history with these people and make sure you're not drawn into extended sales cycles with people who will *never* buy.

The ASK technique (**#18**) can work spectacularly well with revived prospects when you open with a promise and a challenge:

> *"Jim, we spent quite a bit of time working together in Q1, but as I recall you lost your budget. As we're in a new budget cycle, I was hoping that we could try again since we both agreed that my solution could help you. I want to offer my best effort to help you find a way around the budget issues and make you a customer this quarter."*

Collaborative brainstorming with your client to find solutions to their problems always yields good results because they will tell you their constraints and work with you to overcome them. This collective effort has helped me to revive many prospects and convert them into paying customers, but it was usually up to me to initiate this conversation. The beauty of this technique is that you're always building a database of new leads, and this campaign can be initiated every quarter with a crop of new [old] prospects.

Keep in touch because timing and circumstances *will* change, and with a little luck, you'll find that they've changed in your favor.

#29: Hit the Road Jack

There's no substitute for a face-to-face meeting in sales. Hit the road and meet with your best customers and prospects.

In the 1995 movie *Tommy Boy*, Chris Farley and David Spade embark on a nationwide sales trip to save a failing auto-parts company. The beginning of the trip is a disaster and they blow a few sales. As the movie progresses, they learn from their mistakes and their approach evolves. Eventually, they score a huge sale and save the company. Happy ending, roll credits.

I use this example to point out that the main characters don't resolve to hit the phones harder or send more emails when they're in a pinch; **they go on the road and meet with potential buyers in person.** It's been quite a while since I worked in a corporate office, but in those days I would walk past the sales bullpen and listen for two sounds: total chaos or total silence. Total chaos meant the reps were putting in their phone time, which is always important. Total silence meant everyone was on the road, and this is even better. There's nothing more important for a field sales rep than spending time with clients, and I would tell any rep in the home office for more than two weeks to start booking their next trip (and perhaps also invite me along). The reps who virtually lived on the road were usually my top performers.

While technology has given us many more ways to communicate and sell, it's also made the world a little less personal. In the old days, salespeople relied on the telephone and personal meetings to sell their goods and services; no Web meetings, email, or social media. I often traveled with a massive projector (heavier than my suitcase) so I could "plug-and-present" at prospect locations. This was one of the tools of the trade when you sold software in the early '90s, and the plan was simple: work the phones to set up meetings and then hop on a plane to meet with the prospect and close the deal. It was inconceivable to close large deals without multiple trips to see the customer.

Nowadays, it's common for sales reps to close healthy, six-figure deals without ever leaving the office and meeting the prospect. Even field salespeople have become inside reps; scaled-back travel budgets and Web conferences encourage reps to only travel when they have to. While this strategy keeps sales costs down, it loses sight of the fact that sales will always be about developing relationships. While this can be done remotely, it's much more effective in person. **The bottom line is this: there's no substitute for the personal meeting in sales.**

The importance of face-to-face ("F2F") meetings cannot be overstated, as they enable you to build trust, develop more intimate relationships, showcase your personality and expertise, meet multiple stakeholders, and demonstrate to the customer that you actually give a damn about their business.

F2F meetings will help you to:

- Sign a contract
- Meet multiple stakeholders
- Showcase your personality
- Introduce new players (see **#6: New Faces**)
- Observe team dynamics
- Read body language
- Create a shared experience
- Build rapport
- Develop stronger personal and business relationships
- Build trust
- Convey respect
- Show that you care
- Change the tenor and tone of a business discussion

Just because you can close deals over the phone doesn't mean it's always the best way to run your territory or work with clients. **If you truly want to blow out your number, target every single prospect you want to close within the next three to six months for a F2F meeting.** For reps used to sticking close to the office, you'll be surprised at the effect this simple change in tactics will have on your deals.

* GAME PREP *

Business travel requires good planning to be effective. You want to choose the right prospects to visit, build effective meeting agendas, assemble the best resources, and maximize face time with your prospects while minimizing downtime and travel time. I give my reps two main principles to guide their business travel:

1. target prospects that you can close in the current quarter; and
2. look for opportunities where an onsite meeting could prove decisive in propelling the sales cycle forward.

The concept of "nearness to cash" (discussed in **#27: Prospect You're A** Off**) is helpful when planning your business travel. *The quick rule should be to visit any client that you believe you can close in 3 to 6 months.* Meetings with executives, final demonstrations of your product to stakeholders, and joint working sessions are all excellent agendas for the F2F meeting. F2F meetings can also be used as trial closes, because prospects willing to meet with you and bring in other stakeholders are usually serious about doing business with you.

Meetings that build relationships and goodwill are also fruitful. One week every year, I bring my CEO on the road with me to meet with key clients. I can count on my CEO to bring good perspective to the discussion, and my client often invites their top executives as well. It's been a useful tactic to elevate the discussion with clients and position strategic partnerships and large sales opportunities.

Always work out the agenda in advance with your contact. You may need others in your organization to help with preparation or even join you on the road, so finalize an agenda as quickly as possible. This is the age of the team sale; sales engineers, product specialists, managers, and executives may all be called upon to help you close a deal. They'll need plenty of notice to clear their calendars, and you want them to be fully informed and prepared for your meeting. Get your team involved early in the planning, and make sure they have current information and understand their role in the meeting.

Most trips should be planned around one or two "anchor" meetings with your most promising clients. This determines which cities you visit and your trip logistics. When I schedule an anchor meeting with an important client in Chicago, for example, I'll also try to schedule a social event such as lunch or dinner (see **#30: Eat Your Way to Success**) to build more relationships. I'll also call people from my wider prospecting list in Chicago and try to set up quick meet-and-greets at their office or invite them out for coffee. The nature of your relationship changes once you've met someone, so take full advantage of the time between anchor meetings to set up more meetings and shake more hands.

I know quite a few salespeople who schedule their travel so tightly that they head straight from the airport to their meeting, and then back again. This works if your goal is speed, but you're missing opportunities to connect with people in the local market. Unless you're in an area that you visit often, take the day to visit with companies and make personal connections. Your travel should be like bookends to your day: fly out early and return in the evening. The hours in between should be packed with meetings, lunches, dinners and any other opportunities you have to get F2F with prospects and clients.

* SHOWTIME *

Although you may excel on the phone or be the William Shakespeare of emails, F2F meetings truly give you an opportunity to shine and impress your clients. Start with your greeting. Look people directly in the eye and offer them a firm handshake. Greet them by name, and use their name often when addressing them (it creates intimacy).

Give everyone your business card, and ask for theirs in return. When seated at a table, I like to arrange business cards in a pattern in front of me that mimics the seating chart. When someone asks me a question, I can glance down at the cards and address the person by name. Rehearse your presentation beforehand and show up prepared to knock everyone's socks off. If you're traveling with a colleague, ask them to observe and critique your performance.

When appropriate, they can even film your presentation for later study (as we'll explore in **#39: Lights, Camera, Action!**).

F2F meetings are an excellent opportunity to ask the client for a commitment, because it's much harder to tell someone "No" when they're sitting right in front of you. People will blow you off over the phone without thinking twice, but the dynamic is completely different when you're looking them in the eye. This additional pressure can help you to get what you want, and it's one of the reasons that you can often advance your agenda much more effectively through F2F meetings. It's all part of the psychology of selling—something you should understand and leverage to your benefit.

Just as scientists study animals in their natural habitat, observing your clients in their office can reveal quite a bit about the people you're selling to. You can watch the group dynamics as they unfold: who's in charge, who defers to whom, who's fully engaged (or not), who's an ally, and who might be a problem. (You can't *buy* this type of client insight.)

Since you'll be busy running the meeting, ask your colleague to observe the attendees and take notes on what they see. With the prevalence of multiple stakeholders in many corporate sales cycles, understanding personalities and group dynamics can be immensely helpful in your process. Here are five tips to make the most of F2F meetings with prospects and clients:

- **Pitch the VIP**: Address your message to the most important person in the room. Understand exactly whom you need to sell to and make it your mission to secure their buy-in.
- **Keep the room engaged**: If your audience is staring at their phones or computer screens, they aren't paying attention to you. Pull them back into the conversation by asking for their opinion or posing a question. Fortunately, it's a common practice these days to ask participants to turn off their cellphones for the duration of your presentation.

- **Tell stories**: Studies have shown that people even when people have trouble recounting specifics about a presentation, they almost always remember the stories. Use storytelling to make important points more personal and memorable.
- **Beware of provocateurs and ratholes**: We've all had meetings in which a naysayer tried to throw off our rhythm. In the software world, it's usually someone from IT. Be wary and don't let them sabotage your efforts. Similarly, don't let a single individual drag you into exhaustive detail that'll put everyone else to sleep. Be respectful but firm; tell them you'll help them personally after the meeting.
- **If they cancel, it means trouble**: If a prospect cancels a meeting that you've flown in to attend, write them off. Real emergencies aside, this shows a complete lack of professional respect, and your chances of closing this prospect are slim. If you travel extensively, consider trip insurance to minimize potential losses.

#30: Eat Your Way to Success

Food is a common bond that brings people together. Dine out often with your clients, and use this opportunity to build strong relationships that lead to sales.

I've always loved to travel. It's definitely one of the biggest benefits of a career in sales. Although it's not as fun as it used to be (thanks mostly to the airlines), the opportunity to explore new cities and restaurants on the company dime is definitely a highlight for me. The amazing restaurants I discover are often what I remember best about past travel experiences.

Although my wife thinks that I spend my travel time being a tourist, the reality is that most business travel is 99% drudgery: airports, hotels, conference rooms, fluorescent lights. Mealtime is often the only opportunity I have to escape the confines of the office and do something other than work. Meals are also the perfect opportunity to build personal relationships and actually get to know the human beings you're working with. Most companies recognize that the salesforce needs a travel and entertainment budget, and smart reps spend every dime of their T&E budget on their clients. Why? **Because restaurants are where connections are made, alliances are formed, and deals are negotiated and closed.**

The power of food cannot be underestimated. Food is part of our culture, and the centerpiece of many holidays, occasions and get-togethers. It's a vehicle through which people communicate emotions, share experiences, forge bonds of intimacy, develop trust, and create memories. It can be an expression of one's creativity, a comfort in difficult times and a way to explore similarities and build relationships. A fun local restaurant, an exceptionally good (or bad) meal, and an amazing bottle of wine are all experiences you and your companion will recall fondly, like an inside joke. Dining with your clients can be the spark that propels your relationship to an entirely new level. **People do business with people they like**, and restaurants are an ideal venue to build these strong bonds.

I worked once with a large Midwestern manufacturing company that was considering my product for an enterprise-wide initiative. Potentially, it was a huge deal that would make my year, but it was also competitive. My sales engineer and I traveled to their headquarters to present our solution to the evaluation team, which consisted of two gentlemen who were very polite but also hard to read. They offered us no reactions or feedback whatsoever. Their blank looks could have meant we hit it out of the park or fell flat on our faces—*we just had no idea*. After four hours of what felt like a one-sided conversation, we all decided to break for lunch. To our surprise, our hosts offered to join us, and we piled into the rental car and took off.

As their office was rather remote, our options were somewhat limited. We ended up at a small whistle-stop café that nobody but a local would've been able to find. To our surprise, it was a hidden treasure with a casual ambience and tasty homemade sandwiches. The café staff knew our hosts (apparently they ate there often) and within this laid-back and friendly atmosphere they finally started to open up. We talked about football, kids, hobbies, and vacations as we all got to know each other better. When the conversation turned to business, they told us we needed to make our offer more compelling if we wanted their endorsement. They pointed out exactly what changes they wanted to see, and as they continued, a thought occurred to me: *they're telling us exactly how to win the deal.* When we returned to the office, I made the recommended changes and not long after that learned that we had won the business.

It's hard *not* to conclude that this lunch was the turning point in our relationship. We were able to connect on a new level with the people running the project, and this shared experience was key to our winning the business. I'll bet that my competitors didn't create the same opportunity for themselves. I have dozens of stories just like this one, and they all reinforce my conviction to look for every opportunity I can to share a meal with my clients.

I probably receive more emails about this technique than any other, mostly because people have been doing this for years and they can't believe how easy, fun and rewarding it can be. *Cool restaurants, great meals, getting to know my clients better? Count me in!* There's very little downside to a technique that allows you to (1) spend your T&E budget, (2) enjoy a great meal, (3) connect with clients, and (4) let your mask slip a bit to reveal more of your personality to the world.

This technique is so powerful that some of my sales colleagues will arrange their travel plans and meetings specifically to allow for meals with clients. Whenever I'm in New York, one of my clients and I always meet at the same restaurant. It's become our ritual over the years, and I might add that he's also bought more than a million dollars in software from me. We've created a shared experience and become friends, and everyone knows that friends support and do business with each other.

Follow these recommendations and you'll be well on your way to truly **Eating Your Way to Success**. *Bon Appétit!*

- Take advantage of the casual restaurant atmosphere to develop a rapport before you talk business. The more I work with executives, the more I realize that they rarely jump directly into negotiations. Instead, they banter, find areas of common interest and get to know the person sitting across from them. It's much easier to connect on a personal level when you're removed from the corporate environment, and establishing a good rapport will lead to more productive business discussions.
- Choose the right venue. Your goal is a relaxed ambience in which you can have a conversation, so avoid loud music and over-the-top party venues. I once met clients at a Greek restaurant, and we were all surprised when the people next to us jumped up on the table and started smashing plates. Although memorable, it was also a bit hard to concentrate on our conversation.
- Skip the chain restaurants. Ask your contact to recommend a local venue to make your dining experience more memorable.
- Keep costs reasonable. Expensive doesn't always mean better; my café lunch came to $32 (with tip) and led to a

$750K deal. *Pretty decent ROI, yes?* Instead of dazzling the client, overindulgent spending can prompt them to question how your company manages its finances. Keeping your costs reasonable also saves you from uncomfortable conversations with the CFO.

- Inquire about dietary restrictions beforehand: you don't want to bring your vegan client to a steakhouse.

- Watch your alcohol intake. In general, I recommend skipping the drinks at lunch and imbibing with moderation at dinner. Keep in mind that you are out with clients, not your sales team. Drinking too much, even in a social setting, leaves a bad impression, so follow your client's lead and always keep your water glass full.

- When the bill comes, it doesn't need to be an awkward moment. My recommendation is this: always be prepared to pick up the tab. Entertaining clients is a T&E expense, and this money is well-spent in pursuit of your sales goals. Some organizations have clear rules defining what their people can accept from vendors, while others will cheerfully let you pick up the tab every time. I usually ask: "If it's okay with you, I'd like to pick up the tab for dinner," and ask the waiter to bring me the bill. If this is a problem, the client will let you know, but they always appreciate the offer.

PART FIVE

Upsell Your Customers

Without a doubt, your fastest path to short-term revenue is upselling new products and services to existing customers. Developing a smarter approach to upselling your customer base pays well, and is much easier than signing new prospects. The numbers clearly (and dramatically) support this strategy:

- The cost of acquiring a new customer is **five to ten times** the cost of retaining an existing one.
- The average spend of a repeat customer is a whopping **67 percent more** than with a new customer. [8]

Everyone celebrates new logos when a client is signed, but strategic companies—and salespeople—recognize the revenue potential of their customer base and how important it is to long-term growth. In many cases, this has led to a fundamental paradigm shift in the sales organization, with a greater emphasis placed on customer service and the long-term relationship.

While new-business development will always be important to driving growth, you'll see more revenue (and an easier sales cycle) by selling more to existing customers. Your renewed focus on maximizing the lifetime value of the customer can only be successful if two conditions exist: (1) a thriving base of happy customers, and (2) a concentrated effort to expand the product footprint and upsell the customer. The techniques presented in Part Five will make sure you're starting from a position of strength and fully able to maximize the revenue potential of your customer base.

The 6 techniques presented **Upsell Your Customers** are:

---

[8] Inc Magazine (*http://www.inc.com/guides/2010/08/get-more-sales-from-existing-customers.html*)

#31: Pitch the Base
There's no surer path to short-term revenue than selling more to your existing customers.

#32: Check the Vital Signs
A "Health Check" is an opportunity to assess your client's success with your products and upsell new products and services. Make the health check a requisite service for your customers and you'll keep them happy and protect existing revenue streams while creating new ones.

#33: Work the Financial Calendar
Timing is everything, and this is especially true in sales. When you learn how and when your customer makes decisions and moves money, you'll be in the right place at the right time to secure the deal.

#34: Hot Chilies in Your Renewals
When it comes to renewing a customer contract, don't just go through the motions. Instead, seize this opportunity to redefine your relationship, upsell new products and services, and better position your company for future business.

#35: Audit Your Customers
The audit concept is simple: identify customers using more than they're paying for and sell them what's needed to come back into compliance. It's a win-win: you can help the customer abide by your licensing terms while creating new (and unexpected) sales opportunities for yourself.

#36: Open Your Little Black Book
Once customers become ex-customers, most salespeople forget about them. Instead, give them a call and see if you can rekindle an old romance.

#31: Pitch the Base

There's no surer path to short-term revenue than selling more to your existing customer base.

I would highly recommend that any salesperson seeking quick revenue focus on pitching your customer base first. Sales dollars might be incremental and smaller than brand-new contracts, but these deals will close faster and with less red tape.

Unlike new prospects, your customers have already made a commitment and invested in your company. They want the greatest return possible from their investment, and will be inclined to spend more money with you *as long as they continue to see value*. Every salesperson managing a portfolio of customers needs to develop an upsell plan, and there are many options available to you when you're considering how best to **Pitch the Base**:

1. **Increased quantities:** Selling customers more of what they already have is a quick and easy transaction. Increasing a customer's user count from 1,000 to 5,000 users, for example, can result in a significant deal.
2. **Cross-selling:** Complementary products that add value to your overall solution and broaden your product footprint.
3. **Enhanced products:** Upgrading customers from the Basic to the Premium model.
4. **New products:** The launch of a new product should be cause for celebration in the sales department; it's a perfect opportunity for you to upsell your customers and make more money.
5. **Free to Paid:** Upgrading customers from free products to a paid model.
6. **Multi-year upgrades:** Increasing the customer's commitment term (i.e. upgrading from a 1-year deal to 3-year deal).
7. **Services:** Selling the customer related services such as training, consulting, professional services and customization.

8. **Enhanced support:** Moving the customers from Basic to Premium tech support.

It goes without saying that you have a much better chance of generating new opportunities if your company sells a wide and diverse line of products and services. While researching this book, I made a point to reach out to former customers and corporate buyers to get their perspectives on the dynamics of buying and selling. One comment I heard frequently was that although vendors seem to be rolling out new products at an unprecedented rate, they do a poor job when it comes to keeping customers informed and up-to-date. If your customer doesn't know about your new product lines, they can't buy them.

Recently, I read about one company's innovative approach to this challenge, and it began with a simple letter. Every year, this vendor sends their customers a personalized letter listing all of the products and services the vendor provides with the customer's purchases highlighted. Any unchecked boxes are sales opportunities, and two weeks later the customer receives a call from a sales rep asking if they'd like to learn more about how the vendor can help their business. This seemingly simple process generates hundreds of thousands of dollars in revenue for the vendor every year, and costs only a few hours of the salesperson's time.

The more proactive you are in terms of communicating with and upselling your customers, the more success (and revenue) you'll see. Don't wait for them to come to you; actively seek out opportunities to engage and deliver your message.

* GAME PREP *

To develop a proactive and effective strategy to pitch the customer base, your preparation will consist of the following steps:

1. Identifying the customers most likely to buy more from you.
2. Creating the vision and clearly stating the benefits.

3. Formulating an offer with incentives to drive urgency.
4. Pitching the right person who can make a decision and take action.

For the most part, you'll know your A-list customers. They're happy with your company, actively using your products to help their business, and always willing to talk to you. **Call these companies first**. For everyone else, a bit of work is required to find potential upsell opportunities, and this where a customer checklist will prove useful.

To create your customer checklist, start with an Excel spreadsheet listing all the products and services that your company provides. Add a column for each of your customers, and place a check next to everything that the customer already owns. Make sure that the list is current and complete, and includes any options (like multiyear upgrades) that you can sell. As you scan through this sheet, look for unchecked cells. **These are your sales opportunities**, and should be pursued with vigor.

Once you've identified your targets, developing a compelling pitch and offer starts with the consideration of how a new product or upgrade will benefit the customer. Put yourself in their shoes and reflect on what would prompt *you* to action if you were the customer. Think about what my colleague calls "the vision thing": a forward-looking picture of how things *could* be, backed up by solid business rationale. This can build excitement, and your vision statement should clearly state the benefits to the customer *(What's in it for me?)* and the potential results it will generate *(How does it make my job easier?)*

Technique **#21: Let's Make a Deal** explores how to design smart incentives that drive urgency in your sales cycle, and when you combine this with your intimate knowledge of what's important to the customer, you have a winning pitch. You also need to anticipate objections and think about roadblocks that might impede your progress. For example, if you're making a $100K pitch and know your contact has signing authority up to $30K, you can position four equal payments of $25K (instead of $100K upfront) to avoid the additional layer of approvals. As you've sold to your customers before and know how they buy, you can design an offer that's easy for them to accept and move through approvals and purchasing.

Consider the right contact for your sales pitch. Your idea might make all the business sense in the world, but if it's delivered to the wrong person, it may never get off the ground. While many reps like to stay in their comfort zone with people they know, **the best move is to pitch a decision-maker with budget**. If you can't pitch the decision-maker directly, make your case to the people who will directly benefit from a new purchase and ask *them* to sell the decision-maker. You may only have one shot at making an effective pitch, so choose your target wisely. In review, here are the steps to target and pitch your customer base:

1. Rank customers in terms of their level of satisfaction and potential interest in new products and services. Start with your A-list customers first.
2. Create a spreadsheet that compares your full line of product offerings to what each customer has purchased. Any unchecked cells represent your sales opportunities.
3. Develop a strong business case focusing on why a new purchase will benefit the customer. Anticipate customer objections and potential roadblocks to be overcome.
4. Consider each customer's unique situation to customize your offer. Sweeten offers with incentives prompting the customer to move *now*.
5. Finalize your message and determine the right audience for your pitch. You may only get one shot, so make it count.
6. GO FOR IT! Introduce urgency and ask the customer for their commitment.

* SHOWTIME *

Schedule time with the customer specifically to make your pitch. As you apply your own creativity, I'm sure you can come up with many innovative ways to create new sales opportunities within your customer base. Measure your success in terms of deals won and revenue booked, and continue to use the techniques that work best for you. Here are several approaches that I have used successfully to upsell the customer base, and many of these are detailed in the various techniques you'll read about in this book:

- Target happy customers who haven't bought anything from you in a while and/or are using an older version of your product. Call them to extol the virtues of your new product and give them a nudge to buy.
- Ask the customer for 30 minutes to deliver a highly relevant and personalized presentation on your latest product line. Present them with a special offer: i.e. purchase this month and save 10%, or defer payments for 3 months.
- Hit the road and visit every one of your customers. Instead of talking about yourself, research their company and identify one or two pressing challenges that you can help them solve. Create urgency by asking for a commitment to start working with them right away to address these important problems.
- Bring your CEO on the road with you to meet with senior contacts. It's amazing what opportunities can come out of these executive-level conversations.
- Request a meeting with the customer to present five ways that you can help them make more money. Demonstrate clearly how your products will help to launch this initiative and offer resources to help them get started quickly.
- Ask your contact to set up a meeting with their peers in other business units. Present an overview of your solution to the group, and pitch them on the economic benefits of a *joint* investment.
- Run a customer webinar to preview your new product lines. Hold an open discussion and ask for their feedback. Offer all attendees a limited-time discount to purchase now.

A final note: **Every dollar of new business from your current customers will be 100% contingent on their degree of satisfaction with you and your company**. Delighted and engaged customers will continue to invest in you, so always do right by your customers and put their needs first, and you'll be rewarded with an ongoing (and lucrative) stream of deals and revenue.

#32: Check the Vital Signs

A "Health Check" is an opportunity to assess your client's success with your products and upsell new products and services. Make the health check a requisite service for your customers and you'll keep them happy and protect existing revenue streams while creating new ones.

I was first turned onto the concept of a health check while selling software for a startup in Silicon Valley. After seeing the results of this simple but powerful exercise, I've made it a requirement for every one of my sales organizations ever since. The premise is this: a 3 to 4 hour customer meeting with the express purpose of analyzing the customer's use of your products, identifying problem areas, and making recommendations for improvement. While this might seem like a routine meeting, it's actually one of your best opportunities to demonstrate thought leadership, reorient customers headed for trouble, guarantee future revenue streams, and build new sales opportunities within the customer base.

While customers consider it free consulting, I view these meetings as a powerful vehicle to showcase my company's expertise and position future sales. A typical agenda contains three items: (1) a review of the customer's history and current usage; (2) an analysis of this usage by our experts; and (3) recommendations on the right course of action moving forward. Once you diagnose the customer's problems and understand their direction, you're in a perfect position to recommend the right products and services to accelerate these efforts. We'd dig deep into our solution toolbox to bring our full range of offerings to bear to help the customer succeed, and the subsequent deals could be significant. **At one point, close to half of all health checks resulted in new business.** This is a lucrative source of revenue that offers a dual benefit: *helping yourself while also helping the customer.*

Health checks can combine many elements, including analysis, observation, interviews, and surveys. They'll require time from your extended sales and support teams and follow a distinct process flow, beginning with a deep dive into the customer's usage data and environment. We'd pull and analyze all available data and schedule interviews with customer contacts and our own extended teams. If needed, we'd send the customer an online survey. Once the data was collected, our product experts ran their analysis to make sense of it all. This would include **developing an overall picture of the customer's usage and searching for patterns and "blips" that might reveal inefficiencies.**

With a better understanding of the customer's usage, we could apply our knowledge to develop specific recommendations that addressed problem areas and built a foundation for growth. Key to our success was the fact that our recommendations were backed up by the extended team's deep product knowledge and experience gained from hundreds of customer engagements. We came in as experts, and the customer listened to us. We weren't afraid to shine a light on problems and provide an honest assessment. Although the message wasn't always what the customer wanted to hear, they respected our opinion. To present our findings, we'd schedule a half-day onsite meeting with the customer, and, importantly, the executive sponsor.

The strategy for the onsite meeting is to present your findings and conclusions, highlight your recommendations and ask the executive sponsor for a commitment to move forward. The fact that 1 in 2 customers would make a further investment with us is a testament to this approach. Health checks not only generated new revenue, but also helped us identify problems early that might have jeopardized future renewals. This modest investment of our time and effort served to strengthen multiple revenue streams and position our company as a highly customer-focused organization.

If the customer was stalled and struggling with implementation, our task was to get them back on track. If they were preparing for growth, our recommendations focused on how they could scale. At times, customers simply wanted to squeeze more out of their current investment. The point is, there will *always* be ways a customer can improve, and this is what makes the health check such a powerful sales vehicle. There are not many programs your company can implement that will help your customers succeed, protect existing revenue streams, drive new sales opportunities, and improve customer service. The health check does all of these and more.

* GAME PREP *

Is your company set up to run ongoing health checks? This is an upfront reality check as it's an investment that will take time and involve resources from multiple departments. You may want to recruit your sales manager or another executive to sponsor this idea and help you socialize it at your company. Position this as an experiment to generate new business and improve customer results, and when health checks work as promised, you can take full credit for introducing this groundbreaking new concept to your organization.

Who are your most likely candidates for health checks? I recommend starting with companies that you believe could buy more from you (growth customers) and companies currently struggling with your solution (customers in trouble). Growth companies are the most exciting in terms of new revenue opportunities, and their success can create a lucrative revenue stream for you. For companies in trouble, it's more about righting the ship than exploiting growth opportunities, but retaining an existing customer protects your revenue stream and creates future opportunity. Plus, customers in trouble will be grateful for you help, and grateful customers stick by you and may need to spend more money to get well with your solution.

Call the customer to reserve a meeting date on their calendar. You want to position the health check in the right way, so be sure to explain that *it's all about hands-on customer service*. My approach was to explain that it's a best practice for my company to take an in-depth look at how customers are using our products, and then make recommendations on how they could improve. You can even call it free consulting. **It's of paramount importance to have the executive sponsor in this meeting** (more on this later), so schedule meeting dates around this person's availability. *Don't* agree to a meeting unless the executive is a committed attendee.

With your timeline locked in place, you and your team can get to work.

Your prep work for the health check should focus on three areas: analysis, conclusions and recommendations. Analysis consists of both data collection and expert review, and your goal is to generate an accurate picture of the customer's current usage and product environment. Your starting point is to pull together whatever data you have on how the customer is using your products. If you work in cloud-based software (like me), customer usage reports are easy to generate. For other industries, it's likely to take a series of conversations with the customer and your internal teams to develop a clearer picture. Create an interview questionnaire and start scheduling interviews with key contacts at the customer. If you decide to cover more ground with a customer survey, make sure to give yourself enough time to collect and analyze the responses.

Once the data is collected, it's time to bring in product experts, consultants, and support staff to draw conclusions and help you develop a series of recommendations. You want your most knowledgeable resources helping you with this exercise, so recruit your top people to help you. A typical health check will seek answers to some or all of the following questions:

- Is my solution delivering the expected ROI?
- Is it optimally configured for the user community?
- Is the customer pushing the limits of my product, or underutilizing it?
- Is usage even or sporadic, and what do these patterns tell us?
- Is the customer trained on new features relevant to their processes? What percentage of the total capabilities is the customer using?
- Is the right support and training infrastructure in place to fully leverage the solution?
- What best practices can we recommend that would help this customer?
- Do we see any growth opportunities or new applications for our products?

As my team and I assembled a snapshot of the customer's usage, gaps and opportunities would begin to reveal themselves. This, in turn, would define our upsell opportunities: the products, add-ons, upgrades, training and consulting the customer could purchase to help them reach their goals. Your full solution-set should come into play as you develop a "get-well" plan for the customer. **We'd also seek to quantify the cost of inaction.** Customers always had the option of ignoring our recommendations, so we were clear about the implications of doing nothing. When the cost of inaction was substantial, it would inject a note of urgency into our discussions and improve our chances of securing a commitment.

Your deliverable to the customer should be a written health check report that includes the data sets you analyzed, your conclusions, and your recommendations to move forward. **Avoid being overly critical: the purpose of a health check is *not* to point out mistakes, but to offer a thoughtful analysis and a better path forward to increased ROI and efficiencies**. The most effective recommendations lay out concrete steps that the customer can take to get started and make it easy for them to commit. Remember, the customer *expects* your recommendations, and if these result in a sales opportunity for you, it's a win-win. Over time, you can compare past health check reports to more current usage, and this will validate that your customer is moving in a positive direction and succeeding with your solution.

* SHOWTIME *

The health check meeting is your opportunity to shine and highlight your value as a partner. You're introducing potentially provocative concepts, so be prepared for a spirited discussion. The customer may challenge your analysis, dispute your conclusions and downplay your recommendations. I recall having one CIO lecture me for twenty minutes about how his group was "doing just fine" and didn't need my help. It happens, but it's a rarity. I've also had customers invite a dozen people to our health-check meetings, so be prepared to exercise your skills in crowd management if all the stakeholders show up! Prepare a brief PowerPoint deck to help you present your findings and guide the discussion.

I'll illustrate how an effective health check meeting should be run with a real-life example. My team and I showed up at a client's location on the designated day to find eight people (including the executive sponsor) waiting for us. *Big group*, I thought. We kicked off the meeting with a recap of the customer's journey to this point, including why they bought our solution and what they hoped to accomplish. They had laid out very specific goals for Year 1, so our sponsor shared the scorecard he used to track their performance. While progress had been steady, they still weren't quite hitting the targets they established.

Our analysis of their usage data revealed several points of interest, particularly that the biggest group was only using a tiny fraction of the product's capabilities, and two other groups were apparently not using it at all. *This came as a surprise to everyone.* We concluded that among the groups that were using our product, productivity had actually risen, and the non-participatory groups were dragging everyone's results down. Our mission was to sell this story to the executive, because his buy-in was critical if we were to implement our recommendations. To his credit, he was fully engaged and committed to working with us on a solution.

Once we had set up the right conditions for our recommendations, we proposed the following to the executive:

1. Empower the super-user groups with a product extension to enable them to continue to push the envelope, and
2. Hire us to train the slower-moving teams and mentor them in the use of our product over a 3-month period.

As I recall, my pitch went something like this:

"As we can all see, you have several groups outperforming the rest in terms of product usage and results. We need to empower these groups to continue to move forward, because their results are driving the division's overall performance. I recommend upgrading this group to our v2.0 product, and I'm prepared to offer you a good deal on it. To maximize overall ROI, however, you need everyone in the organization working within the

system. To this end, my team can come in for three months, train everyone, and ensure a minimal level of compliance across all teams."

I then looked right at the executive and asked him for his business:

"Dave, I know you've invested in this initiative, and we want to make sure it's successful. Every day we wait means that you're continuing to miss your targets. I can deliver my 2.0 product to you within a week, and we can begin training in ten days. Just give us the word and we'll get started right away."

You need the executive sponsor in the health-check meeting because you want to ask for their commitment to move forward *today*. You've spent weeks reviewing the customer's data, interviewing their people, and working with your internal team to develop an action plan. You've built a strong case backed up with evidence. In my opinion, you've earned the right to put them on the hot seat and ASK for the business. Additionally, if you've been able to quantify the cost of inaction, it will pressure the executive to move with increased urgency.

Dave was a bit surprised at my directness, but I had invested in building this relationship and felt justified in asking for his commitment. He gave me a conditional green light to proceed and asked that we work out several details before final approval. We signed the deal, and it turned out to be exactly what this customer needed to outperform their goals in Year 2 (as validated in our subsequent health-check meeting a year later).

Vendors selling complex products that are difficult to deploy might run quarterly health checks with new customers in the first year. You'll find the right cadence for your organization as you become more experienced with health checks, and you'll also begin to see the benefits of this important technique:

- You're creating new sales opportunities for upsell
- You're being proactive in fixing problems that could otherwise lead to frustrated customers and canceled contracts.

- You're building bridges with the executive
- You have a stage to showcase your company's thought leadership and knowledge.
- You're establishing yourself as a customer-focused company that takes responsibility for their customers' success.

Even though they require an investment of time and resources, health checks will more than pay for themselves and become a staple program in your sales organization. You'll be helping the customer while you help yourself, and this is a winning strategy for *any* sales organization.

#33: Work the Financial Calendar

Timing is everything, and this is especially true in sales. When you learn how and when your customer makes decisions and moves money, you'll be in the right place at the right time to secure the deal.

"I'm a great believer in luck, and I find the harder I work the more I have of it."
- Thomas Jefferson, 3rd U.S. President

One of the best pieces of advice I ever received from a sales manager was to gain an intimate understanding of how money works and moves within my customer's organization. "Follow the money," he advised, "and you'll figure out how to get your share." He directed me to learn how and when the customer does their budget planning; the approval process for purchases; who can say "Yes" (and "No"); spending levels for Directors and VPs; which departments could always seem to find money; and how discretionary budgets worked for unplanned purchases. Armed with this knowledge, I increasingly found myself in the right place at the right time to sign new business. Many of my colleagues called me the luckiest guy in the world, but here's my big secret: luck has very little to do with it.

Timing really *is* everything in sales. We've all had customers tell us how much they love our products, but that "it's just impossible for us to buy right now. Call back in six months." On the other hand, we all get lucky sometimes, and hearing the words, "Fortunately you've caught us at exactly the right time" is like music to a salesperson's ears. Your can transform yourself into the luckiest sales rep in the world if you can gain a good understanding of the relationship between your customers and their money.

While injecting yourself into the customer's budget-planning process will set you up for a sale in the new year, your best bet for quick deals is to call the customer at the *end* of their fiscal year when departments have use-it-or-lose-it budget they need to spend.

No sane manager will return money they can spend on themselves, and this "perfect storm" of leftover budget and timing becomes a boon for the "lucky" rep who has the foresight to call the customer at exactly the right time.

It's a win-win for everybody: the customer gets the products they wanted, you get your deal, and your CFO sees new revenue that has appeared miraculously out of nowhere. These deals can become game-changers for you and your company in slow quarters and guarantee that you end your year with a bang. Let's examine how you can put yourself in the right place at the right time to bring down year-end deals *and* secure a spot in the customer's budget for purchases in the upcoming fiscal year.

* GAME PREP *

Your goal is to nail down the key dates when the customer will be making "buy" decisions so you can get on their radar. To this end, a thorough understanding of their financial calendar and buying patterns is crucial. The questions below will help you to assemble a financial profile of your customer, and should be added to your list of standard discovery questions:

1. When does your fiscal year end?
2. When do you begin your internal budgeting process for the upcoming year?
3. Do unused funds from the current fiscal year roll over into the next fiscal year or revert back to corporate (i.e., disappear)?
4. Who has ultimate authority over purchases in your department?
5. How does discretionary budgeting work for unplanned purchases?

For public companies, read their latest 10-K report to find answers. For private companies, online resources like CrunchBase will supplement your inquiries and help you develop a financial profile. As your knowledge of the customer's buying cycles increases, you'll know exactly when to call the customer and make your pitch. **Avoid the assumption that every company operates on a**

calendar year, as I've actually found this to be the exception. I'd estimate that less than half of my clients actually end their fiscal year in December. It's funny, because nobody can actually tell you why their fiscal year ends in May or October—it's just the way things are.

As important as the *When* and *How* of your customer's finances is the *Who*. You need to know who really controls the budget, who approves purchases, and who needs to say "Yes" along the approval chain. Of equal importance is identifying the people who can say "No," because these folks can kill your deal before you even know they exist. For example, one of my customers required the CEO's EA to sign off on every vendor proposal. If she didn't approve the deal, it didn't happen. I neglected to learn this until my painstakingly-crafted proposal almost crashed on the rocks. Be diligent, ask questions, and use tools like the Close Plan (**#22**) to help you develop a deep understanding of the customer's process.

Your calendar becomes an important tool to help you to time your engagements with the customer. Once you understand their financial calendar, set up two alerts for each customer. The first is a 45-day alert before the end of the customer's fiscal year. This is the right time to begin inquiring about use-it-or-lose-it funds and positioning your products as the best possible use of these funds. The second is a 7-10 day alert before the customer begins budget planning for the *upcoming* year. Your goal is to secure a line item in this budget for your renewal and any new purchases. Don't be afraid to inject yourself into their schedule; this critical period is when you want maximum mindshare as the customer contemplates what they'll be purchasing next year. Sometimes, it's the squeaky wheel that gets the grease.

* SHOWTIME *

While most of *The 40 Best* can be employed at any point to help you sell, **Work the Financial Calendar** is opportunistic and requires you to catch customers at the right time. I make a point to scan several weeks ahead in my calendar every Monday to preview upcoming trips, meetings and alarms that will alert me to an approaching buy cycle. As you can imagine, October and

221

November are excellent months to execute on this strategy. With this in mind, I can plan my travel accordingly and meet with customers at the end of their fiscal year or contemplating next year's budget. I like to make the case for my company face-to-face, and good planning helps me to schedule these important sessions alongside F2F meetings with my hot prospects.

As you begin reaching out customers approach their fiscal year-end, you're sure to find companies with leftover budget to spend. As much as you'd like to think that good timing always wins the day, the reality is that you're probably one of a dozen priorities competing for these funds. You'll be contending not only with other sales reps who actually *did* get lucky and stumble upon this opportunity, but also competing priorities and "pet" projects that employees would like to get funded. Everyone believes that his or her project should get the funding, and it can be a dogfight to win this business.

To make sure the winner is you, you'll need strong internal advocacy and a bulletproof business case. Your champion had better love your product because they'll be required to win this argument with their colleagues who have their own priorities. Invest the time needed to develop a strong case for your deal and equip your champion with everything they need to win. While year-end, use-it-or-lose-it budget may be a windfall for you, that doesn't mean it's easy money.

Leftover budget is not just a Q4 phenomenon: companies that had a tough Q1 or Q2 could be looking for Q3 fixes that will help them post stronger year-end results. This is especially true if your products can deliver immediate benefits on a large scale. I recall selling a large order to a customer that had adopted an "all-hands-on-deck" mentality after a tough beginning to their year; budget was shifted to strategic priorities (like mine) that the CEO believed could impact the bottom line. Fortunately, I was in the right place at the right time, and you can give yourself the same advantage by understanding how your customer plans and spends money. Your sales colleagues may think you have a four-leaf clover in your pocket, but you'll know that you're simply working harder, being smarter, and ultimately generating your own luck.

#34: Hot Chilies in Your Renewals

When it comes to renewing a customer contract, don't just go through the motions. Instead, seize this opportunity to redefine your relationship, upsell new products and services, and better position your company for future business.

In the world of software sales, the typical cadence for renewals goes something like this:

> *A 45-day reminder flashes on my computer screen, informing me that my customer's contract renewal date is approaching. I place a polite call to the customer to make sure that they're planning to renew. When they answer in the affirmative, I draw up an amendment extending their current agreement and forecast the revenue. In 45 days, we sign the agreement, I mark the deal as "Won," and we both move on and forget about it for another year.*

The above scenario reflects exactly how *conventional* salespeople think about renewals. They're happy to get the money with a minimal expenditure of effort. Motivated salespeople, on the other hand, see contract renewals as an opportunity to change the conversation and take their relationship with the customer to a whole new level. **They understand that *any* transaction with a customer is a chance to renegotiate the agreement to their advantage and sell more products**. Standard renewals are boring, but a handful of chili peppers will spice up your renewals and create something far more interesting. Don't be afraid to generate a little heat, because I guarantee that you're leaving money on the table if you're simply going through the motions on renewals.

A winning deal combines good timing with the right offer. From a timing perspective, there is an inherent urgency to renewals: customers must either extend or cancel by a certain date. It's up to you to create the right offer: you can sell the customer more products and services, extend the term of their agreement, or ask them to pay early for an upcoming renewal and pull this revenue forward. Here's an example of how I sprinkled chili peppers on a renewal with one of my clients, a major food company:

The customer's 45-day renewal reminder pops up in my calendar. Before contacting them, I review my notes and account plan. The current contract is for a 2-year commitment, and I'm confident they'll be amenable to extending for another two years. I recall that they'd recently expressed a strong interest in our new "Connect" product, so I make a point to check the current contract to see if we included Connect on their price sheet.

I decide to ask for a longer commitment period and get my Connect product into the customer. I call the VP and make a pitch: rather than simply renewing our 2-year agreement, I propose a 4-year commitment at a 15% discount, saving the client $25,000. As further incentive, I offer them a 6-month free trial of the Connect product in exchange for the 4-year commitment.

I could've just taken down the renewal, which would've been a decent transaction. Instead, I doubled the size of the deal *and* gave myself a very good shot at new revenue in six months when the customer buys Connect. *This* is how you get yourself to President's Club.

Approach renewals with the belief that everything is potentially on the table. In the world of enterprise software, most reps probably do 2 to 3 transactions a year with their best customers, including the annual renewal. It's a perfect opportunity to be creative and ask for more, and shame on the rep who wastes this golden opportunity by just going through the motions.

I've seen a recent trend among software providers, especially in the SaaS space, to pass responsibility for renewals off to the Finance group or junior account managers. This is a huge mistake. Here's an email that I received recently from one of my vendors (who shall remain nameless):

Dear Jonathan Jewett:
Your renewal is due on December 31. Payment is due by this date. Late payments may result in the suspension or cancellation of your service.

It's exactly this level of warmth and personal attention that makes me want to open up my wallet and spend more money with this vendor. *Yeah, right.* You can only imagine how a customer who believes they have a good relationship with your company would receive this kind of message. At their core, renewals are sales transactions, and companies that leave this responsibility to bean-counters and junior reps are leaving money on the table and treating their most valuable resources—their customers—like commodities.

There's an element of hope in the very first sale to a new customer. Neither side can predict with complete confidence whether your product will work as advertised, but everyone certainly hope it will. Customers must put their trust in you to deliver value. But renewals are a different animal because they're based on experience. The customer has used your products for at least a year, and can validate that they work and are producing value. **The act of renewing a contract is, therefore, a vote of confidence in you, and offers you the perfect opportunity to build on this trust to ask for more.**

* GAME PREP *

You need to know the dates of every renewal in your customer portfolio. Set a 45-day alert to remind you when renewal dates are approaching. For happy customers, the renewal discussion is an easy one, allowing you to focus on new upsell opportunities. If I know that the renewal will be a challenge, however, I might begin this conversation a few weeks earlier. Chances are that I'll need this time to resolve the customer's issues and earn back their confidence. Also, because many of the Fortune 500 cling to what can only be described as outdated procurement processes, the sooner you begin the paperwork, the better.

Take a moment to gauge the customer's temperature and state of mind. **Happy customers = excellent targets for upsell and early renewals.** Dissatisfied customers who aren't planning to renew with you = poor targets. Wavering customers who could go either way can = grateful customers, especially when you take it upon yourself to fix their problems. The cost to retaining an existing customer is much lower than the cost to sign a new prospect, so do what you can to keep customers happy and in the fold.

Familiarizing yourself with the customer's current contract and terms is a general best practice, and can give you starting point when considering upsell and renewal options. This shouldn't be hard, because typically you've written these contracts yourself. But, the big question is whether you were paying attention while legal and procurement negotiated the terms buried deep within the contract. I hope you were, because this language can impact your ability to upsell. Fixed price lists, discount rates, free upgrades and service commitments are often negotiated into a contract, and promptly forgotten by the vendor. **But the customer will remember**. A thorough review of the contract is essential to find these hidden "gotchas" and to identify new opportunities for expansion. Contracts are not the most exciting read, but you'll be a hero when you find upsell opportunities that everyone else missed.

As we've covered earlier, the most likely upsell candidates are customers that expressed an interest in your new products. For other customers, you'll want to think about an offer that delivers value and comes wrapped in an attractive package. Scan your product lines and look for **natural extensions and upgrades** to create a compelling offer. People are always interested in upgrades that will make their operations stronger, faster and better. Your customer checklist matching product lines with what the customer has already purchased (see **#31: Pitch the Base***)* is an excellent place to start.

As renewals are essentially future revenues that you are expecting, some companies make it a practice to pull these deals forward to supplement a slow quarter. Your challenge is to make this conversation happen. People are busy and the customer really has no reason to think about a renewal before it's due. You need something that will catch their attention—like the promise of easing their workload. Your buyers may welcome any action that makes their lives easier, and not having to worry about renewing the contract in six months is one less item on their list.

People who may be anticipating changes in their organization may also renew early to secure their own personal interests while they still can. Sometimes you just call in a favor; I've played the relationship card more than once to pull renewals forward when my company needed the money. One final note: check your compensation plan to see how early renewals are recognized and paid out. You'll want full credit and a commission payout when the early renewal closes.

* SHOWTIME *

When your pitch is ready, initiate the conversation with the customer. Email is fine for scheduling a time to talk, but you really want a personal meeting or phone call to make your pitch. Don't be lazy and conduct all of your communications through email! Back-and-forth conversations are fluid, giving you the ability to steer the dialogue and address questions as they come up.

When my 45-day alarm goes off, I reach out to the customer:

> *"Hello Jim, it's Jonathan Jewett. I'm calling because your contract renewal date is approaching, and I want to make sure that we're both ahead of the curve on this. I'd also like to introduce some options that I know will interest you and discuss these before we finalize the paperwork.*
>
> *Since you've been a customer for eight years, I'd recommend looking at a longer commitment term. It will save you quite a bit of money if you were to commit to four years rather than two. Also, you had expressed an interest in our new Connect product. By bundling these options together, I can make you a good offer that'll ultimately save you money and support your growth. I know you're busy, so let me send over some numbers to review. I'll call you tomorrow to walk you through the details."*

Let's examine the dynamics of this message, because there are several tactics at work here that you can use to your advantage:

- **The customer knows I'm looking out for their interests:** I'm on top of their business and remember the renewal before they do. I've been thinking about better ways to work together. I'm proactive in managing our relationship, and ensuring that they are seeing the maximum benefit from my solution.
- **I do all the heavy lifting:** I write the entire proposal; I present a compelling business case; I make it easy for the client to say "Yes."
- **I'm listening:** I remember the customer telling me they were interested in the Connect product, and I've found a way to get it into their hands.
- **I acknowledge that their time is valuable:** This is always a good approach when dealing with *any* customer.
- **I walk them through the proposal:** As mentioned before, I've never been a fan of throwing proposals over the fence and hoping for the best. Walking the customer through my proposal gives me the opportunity to **create the narrative and shape their perceptions to my benefit**.

Per my message to Jim, I'm now on the hook to deliver a proposal. I have a preferred method of presenting proposals to my clients. First, I let them know that my proposal is coming, and schedule a call to review it with them. An hour or two before this call, I'll email the proposal. In this way, they have time to briefly familiarize themselves with the terms, but not so much time that I miss my opportunity to shape their thinking. When we talk, I can spin the narrative in a positive way that supports my interests and preempts any objections.

There are a number of other techniques in this book that can help you to strengthen your pitch and construct a more effective proposal for renewal and growth. Technique **#21: Let's Make a Deal** will help you structure a more compelling offer, while **#16: The Big Audacious Proposal** challenges you to be bold, go big, and sell the vision. For any sales professional, the art of creating a compelling proposal and delivering a highly-targeted pitch should be an area of continuous study and improvement, and renewals are excellent practice.

Although it's simpler than a sales cycle with a new customer, renewals are still a transaction that you need to manage to closure. You may have to sell multiple stakeholders, locate budget, and work through Procurement. The customer has likely budgeted for their current renewal, but funds for new purchases can be a challenge to secure, and this will take time. Nonetheless, renewals present an excellent chance to create new opportunities when you change your mindset and encourage the customer to view your relationship through a new lens.

Let the average salesperson go through the motions when it's time to renew; you can send them a postcard of your toes in the sand at the President's Club beachside resort.

#35: Audit Your Customers

The audit concept is simple: identify customers using more than they're paying for and sell them what's needed to come back into compliance. It's a win-win: you can help the customer abide by your licensing terms while creating new (and unexpected) sales opportunities for yourself.

When I was selling for one of the biggest software companies in the world, the surest path to finding extra dollars to supplement my quarter was to audit my customers for non-compliance with our licensing policy. Because my company compulsively changed its licensing structure, many of my customers were regularly running out of compliance, and this guaranteed that I would find opportunities to "true-up" license counts. No company wanted to be running out of compliance with one of their largest vendors, and their only real recourse was to buy their way back into our good graces. The audit process generated money for my company and commissions for me, and became a reliable stream of new revenue.

Sometimes the customer would contact me to initiate this discussion, but more often than not I'd act on a suspicion that the customer was operating beyond the terms of their contract. This could mean that 5,000 people were using my software when the customer was only licensed for 2,500; other departments were piggybacking on the platform without paying; the customer was using add-on products that they hadn't purchased; the list goes on and on.

When I detected a revenue opportunity, I'd approach my contact and suggest we review their usage data together. Nine times out of ten, I'd find a discrepancy, and nearly every customer would pay rather than scale back their usage. The resulting true-up could generate tens of thousands of dollars in new revenue. The equation is simple: **audits will always uncover licensing gaps, and these become new revenue opportunities when the customer is compelled to buy their way into compliance.**

I'd engage in this dance with a handful of clients every quarter and always find new revenue. If my pipeline was especially anemic in a particular quarter, I simply had to initiate more audits and the revenue would follow. It was a well-known secret that a number of my peers never made a cold call in their life, but instead hit their number by mastering the art of the audit. In reality, nobody really cared *where* the money came from, as long as it continued to roll in.

Compliance auditing is a big stick to wield. Most companies are vigilant about compliance simply because it's the way that they do business. They're fair-minded and embrace business practices that keep them fundamentally honest. For others, it's a question of economics. Violating the terms of a contract can result in penalties and fees on top of the costs required to buy their way back into compliance. In a worst-case scenario, a vendor is within their legal rights to remove their products or flip the master switch and turn the customer off. Although it seldom comes to this, you can imagine how disruptive and devastating this would be for companies dependent on mission-critical systems to run their business.

Sometimes an audit requires your best detective skills, and other times the customer makes it easy for you. I've had disgruntled ex-employees call me up and tell me that their former employer was running out of compliance. These "whistleblowers" will speak freely and tell you who to call and what specific questions to ask. I've even seen postings on social media and blogs that have led me to initiate an audit. While these signals may be faint, it pays to keep your antennae up because they're definitely out there.

The rewards of an audit can be significant. The largest compliance deal I ever signed was for $3M with a healthcare provider. The company isn't around anymore, but at the time they were a white-hot juggernaut in the medical space that could afford to buy their way back into compliance. What began as a routine call led to the disclosure that they had 18,000 people using a product they had licensed for 800 people. This revelation reached all the way up to the CTO, who flipped out and promptly wrote us a check. The resulting true-up became the largest deal I ever closed. As you can see from this example (and many others), compliance auditing works and can generate a big payday.

There is a downside, however. This technique is not for everybody. Audits need to be initiated with extreme care. It's fair to say that not every customer welcomes an unsolicited discussion about their licensing. Non-compliance can result in significant and unbudgeted fees that the customer is compelled to pay. As vendors, we're 100% within our rights to verify that customers are paying us for the products they're using, but it can be an uncomfortable discussion. Be wary of customers using *less* than they're licensed for, because the risk is that they'll turn the tables and want to downsize. This is obviously not your desired outcome, and represents one potential hazard that awaits the sales rep who initiates an audit without the requisite planning.

We all want to maintain good relationships with our customers, so play the audit card sparingly. True-ups are a natural conversation when negotiating new purchases or renewals, but unless they're brazenly flouting your policies, I would *not* initiate audit conversations with any customer more than once a year. Happy customers are worth more to you in the long run than any single transaction, and companies that are made to feel like cash machines will not be your customers for long. Be methodical in your planning and approach and sympathetic to the customer's situation, and you will find that the audit is a big hammer when you need it.

* GAME PREP *

Your first step is to figure out which customers to target. **Random audits are a bad idea**, as this practice will needlessly create negative feelings among your customer base. Your best targets are customers who have informed you that they need more; companies who have aroused your suspicions; and large organizations that restructure often, because they're probably running out of compliance. Audits can also be event-driven in the case of a merger or acquisition. In cases where your company changes its licensing policies, every customer becomes a potential target.

Like any good investigator, you need to assemble the facts and evidence that'll help you develop a picture of the current situation and determine what's needed. An advantage for those of us selling cloud-based software is that our servers track every shred of information about the customer's usage. I can clearly see which customers are exceeding their limits and which customers barely register any usage at all. I can even set up alerts to notify me when overages occur. When the alarm sounds, I'll review the report and place a call to the customer to ensure they're aware of the situation. Chronic offenders are politely informed that they need to upgrade their contract since their current licensing clearly isn't working.

Of course, because most salespeople don't have these kinds of reports readily available, they face the challenge of monitoring customer usage when their products are deployed onsite. It's the "honor system," and the customer is expected to be proactive and notify the vendor when they exceed their limits. Experience shows us that some customers will reach out, others will not, and the majority will be so busy that compliance with your licensing policies is the *last* thing on their mind. The burden is really on you to keep customers honest and identify areas of non-compliance that need to be addressed.

The process begins with your day-to-day conversations with your customers. You need to confirm that customers know what products they currently own and how your licensing structure works. Ask them if they're anticipating any spikes in usage or foresee any big organizational changes. Setting up a Google alert with your customer's name gives you a daily or weekly snapshot of relevant news, and this can tip you off when something big happens that might impact your business with them.

Maintain a customer checklist matching all available products with customer purchases, and make sure the customer has a current copy of this. Also, stay in regular contact with your extended sales team of sales engineers, consultants, trainers and customer-service reps. These people talk to the customers on a regular basis and know when something's amiss. Many audits begin with a tip from your extended team, so confer with these teams often and ask them to stay vigilant.

When it comes to audits, remember the platitude *"Where there's smoke, there's fire."* If you suspect something, follow it up. Look for activities and events that can indicate a change in usage, as all of these can create potential audit opportunities:

- A sudden increase in calls to customer service or support. The customer may be pushing the limits of your products and expanding their usage.
- Customer requests to clarify their current configuration or your licensing policies.
- Tip-offs from your extended team and others close to the customer.
- Events such as mergers and acquisitions, which usually foreshadow a fluctuation in user counts.
- Routine transactions such as new product purchases, renewals and upgrades, which can create an optimal time to inquire about usage and licensing needs.
- Health checks. These are covered in **#32 Check the Vital Signs**, and involve an in-depth analysis of the customer's usage patterns.
- Changes in licensing. Vendors usually don't alter their price sheets to make less money. When you change your policies, call every single one of your customers and schedule time to help them understand the changes and how they'll be affected.

* SHOWTIME *

When you decide to pursue an audit, your first step is to review all available contracts, notes and data to understand the customer's current licensing structure. Be prepared to answer the customer's questions and recommend a course of action to bring them into compliance. When you're prepared, you can initiate a dialogue with the customer. Unlike many other conversations, you actually want to skip the executive, and instead approach the people who are closest to your product, since these individuals are in the best position to validate how it's actually being used. Your approach should be direct and delivered in the spirit of cooperation:

"I was reviewing your usage and it appears that you need more units of our product. That's great news, and it's probably timely for us to discuss your licensing structure. I'll send a detailed spreadsheet with the current licensing filled out, and would ask you to verify your actual usage. Once you've sent this back, we can review it together and figure out what you'll need moving forward."

Be prepared for a range of emotional responses to this message, including surprise, resignation, denial, annoyance and even hostility. Hopefully you've built a strong enough relationship with the customer and presented your case in a constructive way for this negotiation to move forward. I've found that incentives and discounts work well in an audit situation, and can ease the shock of a big compliance bill and help you to look like a good partner. Collaborate with your sales manager to explore these options beforehand. **Your approach should be firm but non-confrontational**, and this will help you to achieve a positive outcome for both parties.

You have a responsibility to your company to ensure that customers are operating in compliance with your policies. People will bargain, plead poverty, ask to downsize, and threaten to cancel their contract. I've seen it all, and my best advice is *not* to back down. Instead, work with the customer to find an acceptable solution. Although auditing is not always comfortable, it *does* work, and can become a reliable go-to channel for new revenue. As your customer grows and matures with your product, audits keep them honest and help both of you to profit from their success.

#36: Open Your Little Black Book

Once customers become ex-customers, most salespeople forget about them. Instead, give them a call and see if you can rekindle an old romance.

The proverbial little black book. . . a physical reminder of memories, people and relationships from your past that just didn't work out. Maybe there was someone else. Maybe you both just changed and grew apart. Perhaps it was a brief but passionate fling, and you both still carry a little spark for each other, just waiting to be stoked.

I'm not talking about your love life, of course, but your former customers. Your professional life is not much different from your personal life in that, over time, relationships come and go. Change is a constant in business, and sometimes these shifts lead to the end of a business relationship. It's unfortunate, but usually not permanent. The executive who canceled your contract moves on. The spending freeze lifts. Your champion takes a job at a new company and they desperately need your product. Assuming that you treated them well, people who did business with you in the past will be inclined to work with you again. It can pay to pull out your little black book and start making calls, because you never know if the conditions are right to rekindle an old flame.

Once I was lamenting a rather slow quarter with my sales colleague when we hatched a crazy idea. We decided to pull the files going back five years and call every single one of our ex-customers. Certainly we had lots to talk about—our new products and services, changes in our company (and theirs), careers, kids, etc. As we began calling, we found some people in the exact same place they were five years ago. Others had new titles, and quite a few had moved on to new companies. We used LinkedIn to update our lists and called as many of our ex-customers as we could track down.

Most people were happy to talk, and in many cases **we discovered that the circumstances that led to the end of our relationship had changed**. One woman informed us that the department head responsible for canceling our contract had left the company, and she had already recommended us to her new boss. Another client had his funding cut, but was just starting a new budgeting cycle and wanted to include us. Others just wanted to see our new functionality and keep in touch. I was amazed by how many ex-customers greeted us with the same remark: "You know, I'm glad you called because I've been meaning to call you…" This informal campaign to our ex-customers ended up generating more than $260,000 in pipeline and $115,000 in revenue within three months. *Wow*, I thought, *not bad for a group of former customers that most people had written off.*

There are many reasons why a business relationship ends, but few of them are absolute. Simply writing off your ex-customers is a big mistake, and too many companies are content to forget about them and move on. **In reality, your former clients are often more promising targets than brand-new prospects, and selling to them is like selling to a customer.** Think about it: the buyers know you and your company, how your products work, and what it's like working with you. They've experienced your value proposition firsthand, and credibility and trust are already established. These inherent advantages make ex-customers low-hanging fruit for the sales organization, and provide more than enough reason to open your little black book and start calling.

* GAME PREP *

Start by generating a list of people and companies to call. Every rep has a CRM system that can easily run reports detailing your former customers. If your business is still transitioning into the digital age, dig through the file cabinet and your old notebooks. Information may be out-of-date, so cross-reference the names on your list with LinkedIn to ensure that your data is current. Don't assume that a new title or company disqualifies someone; most contacts were more than willing to point us in the right direction and make introductions.

It's important to recognize *why* a client stopped doing business with you. I called one ex-customer only to have them inform me that our lawsuit against them had just concluded. *Uh-oh,* I thought, *probably should've done my homework on this one.* To get this perspective, read through your CRM notes and talk to the old-timers; someone will know the reason a customer terminated. If there were bad feelings, legal action or other negative interactions, move on. Disgruntled ex-customers are a dead-end; you want clients who liked you but were compelled by business circumstances to cancel.

Their reasons for canceling are the elephant in the room, and though it may be uncomfortable, you should address these immediately. If they bowed out due to lack of funds, ask if the money picture has improved. If there was a lack of sponsorship, inquire about new sponsorship. If you lost out to a competitor, ask how this vendor is performing for them. You want to find out if the door is open for you—even if just a little—to make a proposal to bring them back into the fold. Of course, the customer will want you to honor their former price point, so familiarize yourself with the terms of their previous contract and consider what you're willing to offer before you speak.

Consistent with our strategy of bringing something new and valuable to every client interaction, consider what will get their attention. Nobody responds well to blatant solicitations that add zero value, and this is especially true for your ex-customers. Open the conversation by informing them that you've introduced exciting updates to your product line or doubled the size of your customer service team—anything that will capture their interest and keep them engaged. I prefer to run ex-customer calls campaigns as a call blitz (**#24: The Call Blitz**), and this means clearing my calendar and making all initial calls within a 1-2 day window. This requires planning and discipline, so give yourself a week to prepare your list and research customers before you start calling.

* SHOWTIME *

While you're engaging your former customers, keep in mind that this campaign may take some time. People are busy, and your priority level has slipped now that you are an ex-vendor. Follow up with these people like you would any other prospect, and expect multiple attempts before you actually connect. On the other hand, chances are good that they'll call you back. When you *do* speak, it's OK to reminisce a bit, but remember that your purpose is to re-sign this customer. You want to get down to business. Here's my "ex-customer campaign" script:

> *"Hello, Kelly, it's been some time since we last spoke. I hope you're well. I remember that your company was acquired and the parent company brought in a legacy platform to replace my product. Now that the organizational dust has settled a bit, I was wondering how this new relationship was working out for you. You may have seen that we introduced a whole new line of products in the past year, and one of these products addressed several areas that I recall were important to you. I'd welcome the chance to catch up, discuss where you are today and see if any of our new offerings could help you."*

Kelly may not call me back because the decision is not hers to make, or perhaps the new vendor is working out just fine. That's life in the big leagues; I update her file and move on. If she does call me back, however, I know she's interested and I can make my pitch. Once you begin talking, it will quickly become apparent whether or not there's a potential sales opportunity. Don't be surprised if the client tells you, *"I'm so glad you called. I've been meaning to call you because the spending freeze has been lifted and I want to request budget for your product. Can you help me work through the numbers?"* Incentives always work when trying to win back ex-customers. **Try offering a special "Welcome Back" promotion that promises to bring back ex-customers at their former price point as long as they sign a contract within two weeks.**

Once your ex-customer is back in your warm embrace, consider how you can protect this business and hedge against disruption.

While changing circumstances brought them back to you, factors like loss of budget or sponsorship, organizational changes, shifting priorities, redundancy and non-performance can send a client packing again. You'll want to identify the risk factors in your customer accounts and take proactive steps to mitigate them.

For example, I recently lost a customer because I had a single champion advocating for my product. When he left the company, his replacement failed to see the value we were delivering and canceled our contract. In retrospect, I should have anticipated this risk and worked to recruit more sponsors across different business units. Instead, I bet this business on a single point of failure (my champion), and his departure foreshadowed the end of our relationship. It was a mistake I vowed never to make again. Most sales organizations have well-documented best practices for account management, and these should include plans to mitigate risk and keep your customer retention rates north of ninety percent.

So, don't toss out away your little black book: keep it handy and open it every so often to call your ex-customers. You'll find it's easier to re-sign an ex-customer than win a new logo, and in many cases you both just pick up right where you left off. Change can be your friend, so keep in touch and wait until the timing is just right to rekindle an old romance.

PART SIX

A Better You

Question: What's the one factor that you have 100% control over in any sales cycle?

Answer: You.

Salespeople are like elite athletes in that we deal with tremendous pressure, perform when the chips are down, and constantly work to improve our skills. In this book, I've included many of the secrets that have helped me (and others) excel in the sales game. The degree to which you're able to produce similar results depends largely on your level of commitment and ability to constantly apply these techniques and sharpen your sales skills.

When wielded by a seasoned rep at the top of their game, *The 40 Best* can be life-changing; a golden ticket to greater riches and a permanent perch atop the leaderboard. If you're just beginning your sales career, *The 40 Best* will accelerate your journey—as long as you commit to an ongoing program of self-improvement and skills development.

A Better You explores how you can expose yourself to the best ideas and people; sharpen your focus; eliminate wasteful activities; become a better speaker; and learn from both victories and mistakes. I believe in the power of positive visualization, so take a minute and close your eyes. Now, imagine your name in lights at the top of the leaderboard. Watch yourself shaking the CEO's hand while you accept President's Club honors (yet again). Picture the biggest commission check you've ever seen. All of this is within your grasp, and *The 40 Best* can become your ticket to ride—as long as you work hard and constantly strive to fulfill your potential and become the best.

There's no greater investment you can make than an investment in yourself, and the techniques in this section will help YOU to make YOU a better and more successful sales professional.

The 4 techniques presented in **A Better You** are:

#37: Steal Great Ideas
Spend as much time as you can with your heroes to learn their killer sales secrets. Then, steal them and make them your own.

#38: Get Lean
Consistently using the Lean selling model will change *everything* about how you conduct business.

#39: Lights, Camera, Action!
Your ability to deliver a killer presentation in front of a live audience is indispensible to your success. Film yourself in action and then watch your movie; you might be very surprised at what you see.

#40: The Power of Reflection
Everyone has room to grow and improve, and most of us could benefit from a self-improvement plan. Start by reflecting on your everyday experiences, because these hold more lessons about how to get better than any other source.

#37: Steal Great Ideas

Spend as much time as you can with your heroes to learn their killer sales secrets. Then, steal them and make them your own.

In 1920, the poet T.S. Eliot published a collection of essays entitled "The Sacred Wood," in which he said: "One of the surest of tests is the way in which a poet borrows. **Immature poets imitate; mature poets steal."**

In 1967, Peter Yates published the book "Twentieth Century Music." In it, he declared the following: "Igor Stravinsky said to me of his Three Songs from William Shakespeare, in which he epitomized his discovery of Webern's music: '**A good composer does not imitate; he steals**.'"

Apple CEO Steve Jobs [inaccurately] quoted Pablo Picasso in a 1996 PBS interview:

> It comes down to trying to expose yourself to the best things that humans have done and then try to bring those things into what you're doing. I mean Picasso had a saying, he said good artists copy, great artists steal. And we have always been shameless about stealing great ideas.

Each of the men quoted above was an omnipotent presence in their respective fields, and they all basically admitted to stealing great ideas from other people. If it works for T.S. Eliot, Igor Stravinsky and Steve Jobs, why shouldn't it work for you too?

In a profession where time is money, salespeople don't always have the luxury to learn as we go. We're expected to get from Point A (today) to Point B (revenue) as quickly as possible, and reinventing the wheel isn't an option. When you can identify best practices embraced by the top performers in your industry and use these to your advantage, there's absolutely to reason to muddle through a lengthy and painful experimentation process. A far better choice is to spend time with your sales idols to discover their secrets and make them your own.

It shouldn't be hard to identify the role models in your own organization because their names sit atop the leaderboard every month. Are these people somehow privy to a treasure trove of inside sales information that nobody else has? Are they literally "born to sell?" Doubtful on both counts. More likely, they rely on a collection of proven sales techniques (like *The 40 Best*) and execute on these better than anyone else.

You need to put yourself in a position to observe the best sales professionals, steal their great ideas, and then make them work for you. It's a proven path to success that spares you the pain of learning everything in your career the hard way.

* GAME PREP *

Start by identifying the right people to observe and study. Whom do you admire in your organization? Who are the sales champions, and would they be willing to let you into their world? Approach these people and ask them if you could ride along for a few days. Let them know you won't be a distraction, but that you're there to learn. Grab the desk next to theirs, or set up a workspace in their office. Schedule time to interview them and ask lots of questions. Sit in on phone calls and tag along on meetings. Any activity that lets you see how this person operates is a worthwhile one.

In many ways it's like new-hire training, but you have an advantage in that you already know the business. In this way, you can hone right in the more sophisticated best practices that truly make this individual stand out. Most salespeople are pretty good at the basics, and it's the advanced tactics that will make the difference in their performance. As for your mentor, most people are flattered by the attention and very willing to help. This process may take you out of your normal role for a few days, but think of the knowledge you'll gain by sitting with top performers and watching them operate. Within a few months, you could be a transformed salesperson.

Before you begin, assess your area(s) of focus and what skills you want to improve. Are you simply looking for good ideas, or focused on specific areas of improvement like the executive conversation and better closing techniques? If you're just looking for overall improvement, any top performer will do. But if you're focused on a particular skill, choose the person who has mastered this skill better than anyone else and persuade him/her to invite you in.

Your task is to observe, so write your observations in your sales journal, and make sure you capture any "ah-ha!" moments for later reflection. **Write everything down**, and keep your journal handy at all times. You never know when inspiration will strike, but it's inevitable when you spend time with people who push themselves to perform at a higher level. These mentoring sessions are most effective when you know what you're looking for, so consider the following areas of focus when developing your observation plan:

- **Time management**: How do they structure their day? What percentage of their day is spent interfacing with clients (important) vs. busywork (less important)?
- **Rapport with customers**: How do they interact with customers and get what they want? How do customers respond to them?
- **Resource utilization**: What people, tools, and other resources do they rely on to help them perform, i.e., their sales machine?
- **Creativity/Innovation**: How do they think outside the box to do their job better? In what ways are they innovative?
- **Adversity**: How do they handle situations like rejection, difficult personalities, tough negotiations, and customer objections?
- **Style**: Is there anything in their personal style that helps them connect with people and achieve better results? This could be their personality, use of humor, subtlety (vs. a direct approach), tenacity, or other qualities.
- **What don't they do?** Almost as important as what they do is what they *don't* do. Top achievers know how to prioritize and eliminate tasks that can distract them from their goals.

- **Secret gems**: The proprietary tips, tricks and techniques that top performers know and use regularly. These killer ideas can be what differentiate the best from the rest, so stay alert and try to pick up on their secret gems.

The mentoring exercise will likely remove you from your normal role for a few days, so it's a good idea to clear this time with your manager. The best organizations invest in making their people better, and the fact that you're taking the initiative to improve your skill-set should be heartily endorsed. After several observation sessions, your sales journal will be overflowing with new ideas that you can use to drive your own success. In fact, sales reps who have followed this program often become mentors for others. In this way, best practices are reinforced and dispersed through the organization, like a rising tide that lifts all boats. Best practice sharing is often they key catalyst to creating a vibrant salesforce filled with overachievers.

* SHOWTIME *

The key to finding value through mentoring is to first observe the best practices used by others, and then look for ways to put these ideas into action. It's easy to watch your colleagues go about their day; what's more difficult is translating these observations into practical techniques that you can apply to your own sales efforts. You won't just be handed the answers to the test; you need to work for them. Below are my notes from one of my mentoring sessions, and you can see that they're a mix of observations, reflections, guidelines, and sales philosophy:

- *Be bold and ASK for the business*
- *Sales is about asking the hard questions. Don't avoid asking hard questions because I may not like the answer. If there's going to be a letdown, find this out before I invest my time to win the business.*
- *Chris doesn't check email first thing in the morning, but waits a few hours before even opening his email. Why? He wants to get started on his own plan in the morning, not be forced to react to emails. He thinks it makes him more productive. Could it work for me?*

246

- *When dealing with a new contact in procurement, engage them in a friendly, personal conversation before getting down to business. This small bit of goodwill will carry over into our business dealings.*
- *Chris disciplines himself to make five cold calls per day. No excuses.*
- *Create an account plan for existing customers detailing the upsell strategy and specific goals. Share this with the extended team (services and support) to make sure they're aligned with my strategy to upsell the customer.*

I chose this particular journal entry because many of my observations are reflected in the techniques I've written about in this book. Consider the entry: *Be bold and ask for the business.* How do you make the concept of boldness actionable? It's more of an attitude than a best practice, so how do I apply it to my sales approach? My answer was to create two techniques—**ASK for the Business** (*#18*) and **The Big Audacious Proposal** (#16)—that build upon the notion of boldness in sales. You're likely to face the same challenge as you observe other people at work, and this is why it's important to take good notes and review/reflect on these at a later time. Observation is easy; what's more difficult is making these lessons actionable and figuring out ways to use them to your advantage. Once you figure this out, these sessions will become invaluable.

If you're in an environment where there are no seriously great role models to observe, you'll need to look elsewhere. If there's a co-worker from your past that you admired, call them up and ask for their sage advice. I subscribe to a dozen sales newsletters written by industry leaders, and these provide valuable tips and insights to help you improve. Organizations like Salesforce.com sponsor virtual conferences featuring thought leaders, authors, and speakers from the sales profession. Look at your partner companies, and ride along with one of their top people. You have to be imaginative and take the initiative to find and steal great ideas.

There are no points awarded for originality in sales—only for results. You should never be shy about seeking out and stealing great ideas. It was a revelation when I first realized that I didn't need to learn every lesson the hard way, but that I could learn from others who had walked the same path before me. As I grew more experienced and confident in my own abilities, I'd refine the best practices I learned to better suit my own style. *This* is how you truly make an idea your own, and don't be surprised if others in your organization want to observe *you* and start stealing *your* good ideas. In fact, you should be flattered. Nobody has an exclusive license on great sales techniques, and we salespeople need to share and work to help each other out.

Although it may be the strangest advice you've ever received, go forth and steal!

#38: Get Lean

Consistently using the Lean selling model will change everything *about how you conduct business.*

"We are what we repeatedly do. Excellence then is not an act, but a habit."
- Will Durant, *The Story of Philosophy*

Lean manufacturing—or just *lean*—is a production philosophy whose mission is to identify and eliminate any expenditure of resources that does not directly create value for the customer. In the lean world, value is defined as any product or service the customer would be willing to pay for. Thus, any process or activity that does not add value is eliminated. The end goal is an extremely efficient system in which all resources are pointed toward a common and clearly defined goal and the individual is executing only on those activities that add value.

Lean principles are derived from the Japanese manufacturing industry, particularly the Toyota Production System ("TPS"). TPS sought to reduce three types of waste: *muda* ("non-value-adding work"), *muri* ("overburden"), and *mura* ("unevenness"). The TPS system was a primary driver in Toyota's exponential growth from a small regional company to one of the world's biggest automakers and brands. I point to the lessons of lean manufacturing because these principles can also be applied to sales. If we were to call our system "lean selling" and define its key principles, our mission statement might read something like this:

The mission of lean selling is to minimize or eliminate any activities that do not (1) serve to delight your customers, or (2) generate new sales revenue.

Think about this concept for a minute, because it has the potential to completely change the way you work. A commitment to lean selling requires that you apply these principles to every activity, every day. It requires that you say "No" to certain customers and eliminate activities that don't meet the lean criteria. At first this will be difficult, but as you become a more disciplined practitioner of lean selling, you will see the benefits of an approach that distills sales down to its two most important principles: **the customer** and **the deal**.

To a large extent, the adoption of lean principles within the sales world is inevitable. Customers are more demanding, and salespeople are busier than ever. When we're not on the road meeting with customers and prospects, we're on the phone, running virtual meetings, demonstrating our product, sending email, writing proposals and coordinating internal resources. When you add in the demands of social media and a personal life, the result is a schedule that leaves zero room for activities that don't directly nurture your health, wealth or spiritual mojo.

As a manager, one of the primary messages I hammer home is the need for my reps to be absolutely *ruthless* with their time. **A salesperson's most valuable resource is time, and there are a million ways to waste it.** I'm constantly amazed (but no longer surprised) by the time that my least-productive salespeople spend on low-yield activities that don't serve to delight the customer or produce revenue. These usual suspects include:

- Crafting and sending massive quantities of introductory emails.
- Pursuing companies that don't fit the ICP.
- Spending too much time with junior-level people who aren't influencers or buyers.
- Pursuing unqualified prospects looking to merely educate themselves rather than buy.
- Running repetitive product demonstrations.
- Overreliance on social media.
- Performing endless research and study.

I think of these activities as being the government bonds of the sales industry: safe, but producing an underwhelming return. I guarantee that your top producers are not focusing on these tasks, but have shifted instead toward a lean-selling model that emphasizes revenue and customer satisfaction as the benchmarks of success. Beginning your own transition to lean selling requires you to examine your goals and activities, prioritize high-value tasks, and steadily eliminate *muda, muri* and *mura* in your daily routine.

* GAME PREP *

It's been remarked that you're not selling unless a prospect is aware of you. . . well. . . selling. Everything else is preparation and practice. Start a page in your sales journal devoted to tracking your daily activities over a week's time, and classify every task as high- or low-value. I've created the following buckets to analyze where I'm spending my time, and prioritized this list from the most to the least important:

1. **Customer interactions:** Meetings, demos, phone calls, prospecting, customer service calls and activities.
2. **Deal mechanics:** Writing proposals, contract negotiations, analyzing current contracts for upsell potential.
3. **Customer prep:** Account planning, creating presentations, strategic planning, market research.
4. **Skills & Brand Development**: Training, mentoring, practicing my pitch, writing articles and blogs.
5. **Everything else**: My catch-all for every activity that doesn't fit into one of the other buckets. This is a good place to start when seeking to eliminate your own personal *muda, muri* and *mura*.

You'll notice that customers and current deals are my highest priorities, and this should be the case for all salespeople. I challenge anyone to name a more important activity in sales than delighting the customer or driving new revenue. Although skills and brand development are lower on the list, both contribute to my long-term success and are, therefore, worthy of my time (assuming they don't infringe on customer or deal activities). Per the tenets of the lean selling model, low-value activities in the "everything-else" bucket are probably wasteful and can be eliminated, thereby freeing up more time for customers and deals. You can begin to see how the lean-selling model brings greater focus to your efforts and ensures that time is dedicated to activities that truly support the sales mission. The extent of your success will be determined by how well—and consistently—you can execute.

* SHOWTIME *

The three pillars of better execution are: (1) a clear definition of goals, (2) defining the right activities to drive goal achievement, and (3) establishing metrics to measure your progress. In the lean system, we know that our goals are to delight our customers and produce more revenue. We know that more customer interactions, meetings, and proposals are the right activities to get us there. The metrics to measure our progress are total revenue closed, pipeline created, and shorter sales cycles. At this point, our task is to examine and refine our process to ensure that we're continuing to move in the right direction and execute at a high level.

To do this, set quantifiable goals for yourself and compare these to your results. Make sure that your goals are realistic and achievable, and use tools like Excel to create trend lines showing your progress. If you're doing well, you'll see more positive trends and results over time, and the obvious conclusion is to continue doing what you're doing. If you're underperforming, figure out why and make adjustments.

Seasoned reps following a lean-selling model are conditioned to ask themselves four questions before they begin a task:

1. Does this activity serve to delight my customer or produce new revenue?
2. Will it contribute directly toward the achievement of my goals?
3. Does it improve my chances of making more money?
4. Do I have to do it?

Questions like these act as a useful filter to ensure you stay focused on the right activities, and I'd advocate the same filters be applied to meeting invitations. Pose the four questions and make sure the they're answered to your satisfaction before you accept the invite. Of course we all have mandatory commitments that fall outside of the lean framework, so take care of these compulsory activities before turning your attention back to your highest priorities.

We discuss the concept of *nearness to cash* in **#27: Prospect Your A** Off**, and it's a useful spot-check of your activity in the world of lean selling. Salespeople are measured by the amount of revenue they produce, and nearness to cash requires you to prioritize any activity that will move you closer to generating revenue. Simply put, **if it's going to make you money, it's important. Deals that could close next week are more important that deals forecast six months out.** Customer meetings, negotiations, product demonstrations, and proposal generation are all near to cash; they're requisite steps in the closing process. Writing blog posts and sending mass email are further from cash, and therefore lower priorities. With these considerations in mind, you can now add a fifth question to your lean checklist:

5. How near to cash is this activity?

A good rule of thumb is this: **If the work involves a call, client, negotiation, contract or meeting that will produce revenue in the current month or quarter, it's important. Everything else can wait.** You'll immediately see a difference in your calendar as you begin to prioritize high-value meetings and tasks. You'll have more confidence in your daily work and the contribution it's making to important goals. Finally, you'll eliminate more of the low-value activities that can overwhelm a salesperson without producing a return. With your highest priorities listed first, a typical day might look like this:

Committed Deals (nearest to cash)
- Revise contract for Client A
- Call executive sponsor @ Client B and ASK for the business
- Schedule time to develop a close plan with Client C
- Coordinate call with the Legal dept. at Client D

Delight the Customer
- Track down bug fix for Client D
- Research pricing for additional licenses for Client E

Fill the pipeline (prospecting)
- Finish calling list of ex-customers
- LinkedIn prospecting for new clients
- Networking event in the city

Recalling Will Durant's quote that excellence is not an act but a habit, lean selling must be a daily commitment requiring self-discipline, repetition and vigilance. As you question every task and activity, important priorities will rise to the top while low-value activities are pushed down or out. Keep at it, and before long you'll become a lean, mean, lean-selling machine.

#39: Lights, Camera, Action!

Your ability to deliver a killer presentation in front of a live audience is indispensible to your success. Film yourself in action and then watch your movie; you might be very surprised at what you see.

In business school, I took a course called "Effective Business Presentation." One of the course requirements compelled every student to deliver 10 presentations in front of the class during the semester. Each presentation was filmed and added to our personal film library, and our assignment was to watch these videos and critique every aspect of our performance. The goal was to observe a marked improvement from Week 1 to Week 10 and closely track our evolution from unpolished to more confident and effective public speakers.

By then, with eight years of real-world sales experience under my belt, I fancied myself a pretty decent public speaker. I felt at ease in front of people and had pitched my products countless times to large audiences. I'd even attended several Toastmasters' meetings to work on my delivery and style. Nonetheless, I was stunned by the video of my first recorded presentation.

I appeared to have an uncanny fear of silence, and either rushed into my next point or used filler words like "um" and "ya know." No exaggeration—during one presentation, I counted 40 "ums" before I became too depressed to keep counting. Moreover, I paced along the stage like a tiger, barely making eye contact with the audience. Instead, I stared at the PowerPoint slides projecting onto the screen. I also noticed a nervous tic; I'd place my hands on my hips and shift from one foot to the other, like a cobra swaying to a snake charmer's *pungi*.

In short, it was a disaster. I then wondered just how many previous sales presentations I had totally blown, and this thought was depressing. **The crux of my problem was that my poor presentation skills took away from the effectiveness of my**

255

message. Although I made good points, they were not delivered in a compelling or memorable way. Just because I thought I was comfortable with public speaking, I assumed this translated into success. *Man, was I wrong.* Delivering an effective business presentation is as much about connecting with people and making your speech memorable as displaying a cool exterior.

In sales, we're constantly called upon to stand in front of an audience and deliver a pitch. Some of us also speak at events and trade shows. **This is your opportunity to shine; your ability to deliver a killer presentation correlates directly with your ability to succeed in sales**. I had seriously overestimated my effectiveness, and the video confirmed that I had a long way to go. I couldn't help thinking back on all those deals that didn't close and wondering if my cocky but underwhelming presentation style was to blame.

Fast-forward to the end of the semester and my final taped performance. The difference from Week 1 couldn't have been more pronounced. I had stopped using filler words; I couldn't count a single "um" or "ya know." I was interacting with the audience; asking them questions, soliciting their opinions, and drawing them into my speech. I lost my fear of natural pauses, and instead used them to emphasize important points. By becoming a more effective and self-assured speaker, I was able to deliver my message with more power, and I couldn't wait to try out my new skills on prospective customers.

Nobody works in sales to lurk in the background; we're always on the front lines representing our company and interacting with customers. Along with the ability to close business, delivering a killer presentation is one of a salesperson's most important skills. That said, *how many salespeople have actually taken the time to watch and critique their performance?* NFL players and coaches spend countless hours reviewing game film to assess strengths and weaknesses and prepare for the next game. Why shouldn't the discipline of film study also work for salespeople?

In this age of the overworked and impatient buyer, you may have only one shot at converting initial interest into an active buying cycle. You need to hook the buyer and make them want more. People can read about your products all day long, but your pitch is really what can make or break an opportunity. A nervous and unpracticed speaker dilutes their message, while confident salespeople can deliver a highly effective message with conviction. It's time for you to bring the power of film to your sales efforts, so hit 'Record' and let's get started.

* GAME PREP *

First off, you want to take advantage of every opportunity you have to film yourself in front of a live audience. Camera phones and handheld video cams make this easy, and it's not unusual for people to film a business presentation. You'll need help with this, so ask your sales assistant or team member to act as camera operator during your next presentation. No need to wait if you don't have any presentations scheduled; practice by recording yourself delivering a 15-minute speech to a colleague. Live settings are always preferable to capture the "live" dynamics, but don't feel as though this is your only venue for learning and practice. When you can, ask your colleagues to review your videos and provide feedback; their view will be more honest and objective than your own.

Your initial goal is to build a library of filmed speeches and presentations that document your evolution as a speaker. You can then study your films and develop a personal action plan that focuses on specific areas of improvement. Developing your public speaking and business presentation skills is a long-term journey, so concentrate on the areas requiring the most improvement first, work at these until they're perfected, then move on to the next set of priorities. I've compiled a list of specific areas that you might decide to focus on as you watch film and build your plan, and these include:

Overuse of filler or "garbage" words: *Um, uh,* and *you know* are garbage words because they add nothing to your message. It's common for speakers to use these while their brains transitions from one thought to the next, but excessive usage will expose you as a nervous speaker. Be aware of triggers that can cause you to use these, and set a goal of *zero* garbage words in every presentation.

Physical presence: What're you doing with your hands? Do you stand still or pace like a caged animal? Do you have any nervous tics, like playing with props or rubbing your chin? Every movement sends a signal to the audience; physical actions need to reinforce your message, not detract from it.

Audience connection: Do you deliver a monologue or get your audience involved? How do you make sure you're memorable? Do you use humor to make people laugh, or challenge the audience with provocative statements? An engaged audience will absorb your message, so explore ways to draw them in.

Messaging: Do you get right to the point or meander? Are you emphasizing and repeating key points to make sure they sink in? A popular approach is to first mention your important points, reinforce them throughout, and repeat them at the end. Find the cadence that works best for you.

Pauses: Many people fear silence and rush to fill the void with garbage words or mindless blather. Natural pauses can highlight key points, encourage questions, and even keep the audience a bit off-balance. Good speakers use pauses to their advantage.

Storytelling: Storytelling is an important skill in sales, and I'm a big believer in using stories to reinforce my message. When you think back to memorable presentations, it's likely the stories that you recall first. Narratives about your customers are always a winner.

Humor: Humor is one of the most effective techniques available to connect with and engage an audience. Make people laugh, and they'll pay attention.

Slides and Props: If you're employing slides, follow Guy Kawasaki's 10/20/30 Rule of PowerPoint: ten slides, twenty minutes, and no font smaller than thirty points. Make sure you're not fiddling with notecards or the projector remote during your presentation; it makes you look nervous and distracts people from the message.

Volume and voice projection: Volume helps you to grab the audience's attention and emphasize your most important points. You're projecting your voice properly when the people in the back row can hear you clearly.

Closing: Reserve two minutes at the end to make your pitch and repeat your key points. End with a bang, not a whimper.

* SHOWTIME *

As you begin to critique your own style, study the masters who are widely acknowledged to be exceptional public speakers. Watch Steve Jobs introduce the iPod in 2001 or the iPhone in 2007. TED Talks have become very popular, and these speakers are usually outstanding. You can watch hundreds of TED Talks on YouTube and critique each presentation using the same criteria you're applying to your own performance. There are many famous political speeches that combine powerful words with memorable delivery, and politicians like Winston Churchill and Barack Obama are well-known for their powerful oratory skills. Once you study the masters, you can set a goal for yourself and measure your progress.

Put yourself in the seat of an audience member and view your performance from their perspective:

- Did you sell yourself?
- Did you convey meaningful points and do it convincingly?
- Did you look comfortable?
- Did you establish a physical presence that pulled people in?

When you watch experts like Steve Jobs, his use of slides is minimal, yet the audience hangs on his every word. *He* becomes mesmerizing. This is the gold standard in business presentation and a high bar to set, but you might as well shoot for the stars and see where you land.

Take notes while watching your videos and keep a journal of your progress. You'll begin to see patterns—both good and bad—and develop a sense of your own style. When you're ready to create your improvement plan, pick two improvement areas to start. Most of us have more than two deficiencies that need work, but it's important to make steady progress and not take on too much at the beginning. I know this from experience: after watching my first performance in class, I wrote down *seven* major problems that I needed to fix. My second presentation ended up being even worse than my first. Why? I became so distracted trying to remember what NOT to do that I completely blew it.

Choose your most glaring problems and work on these first. When they're perfected, pick two more. Practice and repetition are key; you want good habits to become automatic. Over time, you'll see major improvements as you begin to evolve into a more effective speaker and presenter. If I were to put my finger on one single factor that defined my progress as a speaker, it would be confidence. The most compelling speakers possess an unshakable belief in themselves and their message, and this can't be faked—only earned. Once you've given a thousand presentations before a thousand audiences—not all of them friendly—you're pretty much prepared for anything that audience #1,001 could throw your way.

In the age of slashed travel budgets and Web meetings, your ability to deliver a killer presentation *virtually* can be just as important as a face-to-face presentation. The good news is that these skills are universal. Whether it's a Skype videoconference, phone conference or Web meeting, you ability to connect with the audience and deliver an effective presentation remains key to your success. Most virtual meetings can easily be recorded, so you should have plenty of videos to study and review.

As you progress with **Lights, Camera, Action!**, watch your earliest videos and compare these to more recent performances. For many people, the transformation is astounding, and will really highlight your progress. So, flip on the switch, smile for the camera, and bring a little Hollywood magic to your sales career.

#40: The Power of Reflection

Everyone has room to grow and improve, and most of us could benefit from a self-improvement plan. Start by reflecting on your everyday experiences, because these hold more lessons about how to get better than any other source.

There's a *New Yorker* cartoon in which a stylish couple is sitting together in their living room. It's inferred that the wife has just quoted Socrates, "*The unexamined life is not worth living,*" and the husband's response is the cartoon's caption:

> *Him:* "On the other hand, the examined life doesn't seem to produce much income."

This is another instant classic from *The New Yorker*, and, like many of their cartoons, becomes a sardonic commentary on our money-obsessed culture. I must say, however, that I disagree with the husband: the examined life *does* produce more income.

When speaking to a group of sales professionals, I often ask them to raise their hands if they believe they're operating at 100% of their full potential. Usually not a single hand goes up. This naturally leads to a follow-up question: *So, what's your plan to do better?* When people actually provide answers, they mention more training, classes and education, and even yoga and meditation. While each of these is a positive step, they miss a crucial piece of the self-improvement puzzle.

A year spent selling will give you more sales education than reading every book ever written (with the exception of *The 40 Best Sales Techniques Ever,* of course). Your daily experiences battling with customers and pursuing prospects is really how you learn to sell. In this way, every call, meeting and discussion contains insights to help you improve. *Your challenge is to mine these daily interactions and make them actionable.* I call this **The Power of Reflection**, and it's a concept embraced by many business leaders at the top of their profession. When people make a concerted effort to reflect on their performance, identify important lessons, and make improvements, the exercise can be transformative in terms of unlocking one's potential and reaching greater levels of career success.

* GAME PREP *

Most of us probably can't recall the last time we gave ourselves permission to lean back in our chairs, put our feet up, and think about our job performance: how well we did in the big meeting last week; how we handled a difficult situation with a prospect; the mistakes we know we made; and the things we think we did well. In today's hectic business environment, these events fly by with little or no scrutiny, and we miss the opportunity to mine these activities for important insights and lessons.

I first became interested in this reflective power after reading Dale Carnegie's indispensible book *How to Win Friends and Influence People.* Carnegie relates the story of an influential Wall Street banker who attributed his considerable success to a homegrown system he developed and followed religiously. On Saturday nights, he'd retire to his study with his appointment book and review all the meetings, interviews and discussions that had taken place the previous week. For each event, he'd ask himself the following questions:

1. What mistakes did I make that time?
2. What did I do that was right—and in what way could I have improved my performance?
3. What lessons can I learn from that experience?

In the banker's own words:

> This system of self-analysis, self-education, continued year after year, did more for me than any other one thing I have ever attempted. It helped me improve my ability to make decisions—and it aided me enormously in all my contacts with people. I cannot recommend it too highly.

Wow—that's a powerful endorsement from a very credible business leader, and his words made me think. I knew that I had potential and room to grow. I knew that I was making and sometimes repeating mistakes, but I still lacked any kind of cogent self-improvement plan. The banker's system seemed simple and worth a try, so I resolved to follow this program for two months to see how it worked.

The time commitment was minimal; one hour every week for dedicated reflection sessions. I reviewed every meeting and presentation on my calendar, and asked myself the same three questions. Here are the notes from a session reflecting on two F2F meetings and a phone call:

Meeting #1

Brief: A F2F meeting with a prospect to convince the team to move forward exclusively with my company rather than issuing an RFP.

What mistakes did I make that time?
- Not enough due diligence on the competition; an inability to clearly state the differences between my platform and competitive offerings.

What did I do that was right—and in what way could I have improved my performance?
- Good job convincing the executive that RFPs are an expensive and time-consuming process. I also pointed out that time spent administering an RFP is less time spent addressing urgent problems. (They seemed to buy it.)
- It was a good idea to call and lobby several key sponsors before the meeting. Their support for my go-forward plan made a big impression on the executive.
- To improve, I could have provided real RFP costs from current customers. This would have supported the business argument to skip the RFP entirely.

What lessons can I learn from that experience?
- If I can make a compelling case to a prospect to buy from me rather than issuing an RFP, this always works to my

advantage. It'll position me as the front-runner and undermine my competitors.
- Lobbying *does* work, so get on the phone and secure support before meetings.

Meeting #2

Brief: My first meeting (as a manager) with the board chairman and the executive committee to discuss goals for the upcoming year.

What mistakes did I make that time?
- I felt intimidated in my first meeting with the "big guns." This led to my being silent on some occasions when I should've spoken up, and to my agreeing with some assertions that I didn't really endorse.
- I have a tendency to answer questions too quickly. I need to pause and think about my answer first. *Think before I speak.*

What did I do that was right—and in what way could I have improved my performance?
- I was well-prepared with documentation and my proposal was solid. Several people commented on this. In the future, print out paper copies of my proposal so people can mark it up and take notes.
- *Always* approach an executive audience with a solution mindset. No complaining.
- To improve, I should have scheduled 1-1 conversations with each attendee *before* the meeting. Some people changed their positions, and this caught me off-guard. If I had talked with them earlier, I would have known what to expect.

What lessons can I learn from that experience?
- I'd feel less intimidated and more assertive if I knew the executives better. I need to look for opportunities to build bridges with these people.
- Watch the other department heads to see how they present their proposals and themselves. I'm sure there are nuances that I can pick up and use myself.

Meeting #3

Brief: Phone call with a new customer who just signed and now wants to delay their implementation for eight months. This means no revenue for the company and no commissions for me.

What mistakes did I make that time?
- I [uncharacteristically] lost my cool, and was a bit terse with the customer. This set a bad tone for our discussion, and prevented me from achieving a good outcome.
- I shouldn't have mentioned the legal enforcement option; it did nothing to improve the tone of the call.
- I should've come more prepared with contingency plans and a spirit of cooperation: *let's figure out a solution together.*

What did I do that was right—and in what way could I have improved my performance?
- It was a good idea to review the contract beforehand, and it helped me to cite specifics and build my case.
- I encouraged the customer to talk by asking about the challenges that would delay the implementation. I asked them to provide their perspective on our impasse.
- I let the conversation turn ugly because I was angry that the delay would cost me personally. To improve, I need to make sure that I keep it professional and separate personal feelings from my business dealings.

What lessons can I learn from that experience?
- If I'd made more of an effort to speak with the decision-maker, I might have uncovered the customer's lack of readiness. Next time, I'll initiate this call to discuss the go-forward plan before the contract's signed.
- It never pays to show your anger in a business meeting. I need to recognize situations where my personal and professional emotions might intersect, and make sure to keep them separated.

As you can see, reviewing just *three* of my meetings over the past week provided a wealth of information that I would have missed otherwise. We all have flashes of insight that occur when we're sitting in a meeting, lying in bed, or brushing our teeth; that's how the subconscious mind works. The problem with these moments of brilliance is that they're shooting stars: amazing, but quickly forgotten as more pressing priorities take over.

When you set aside time for reflection, everything is written down and you ensure that nothing's lost. Remember that your brilliant insights are somewhat useless without an action plan that leads to actual improvement, so let's explore how you develop this plan.

* SHOWTIME *

As I continued with my weekly reflection sessions, I began to realize that developing insights was only half the battle; I still needed to apply this knowledge and measure my progress. To this end, I created an **Improvement Plan**. At the conclusion of each session I'd pick the most important insights, lessons and theories to be tested and write these on a separate page under the header *Improvement Plan*. Rather than pore through all my notes before a meeting, I could flip to my *Improvement Plan* and quickly scan for relevant points. I'd spend five minutes reviewing the plan before every call and meeting, and look for opportunities to apply these lessons.

I also prioritized the outcomes that I was working towards to keep me focused and help me measure my progress. My self-improvement priorities became:

1. Eliminate stupid mistakes that are easy to correct (small wins).
2. Identify best practices that can be applied to current deals.
3. Identify fundamental shifts in sales strategy and philosophy that will ultimately make me a better salesperson.

With the process and structure in place, my final step was to create a system to measure my progress and track my overall growth. For the most part, my success was subjective, but goals like *speed up*

266

the sales cycle were easier to quantify. Another measure of my progress was the fact that these sessions became less painful as I recorded more successes and committed fewer mistakes. **Ultimately, the final measure of any sales improvement program is revenue. If your plan is working, you'll be making more money and bringing more predictability to your deals.**

As my confidence and success continued to grow, I knew that I was improving at my job, and the numbers backed this up. My personal experience with weekly reflection sessions made me a believer, and it's become a cornerstone of my self-improvement regimen that continues to this day.

There's nothing more frustrating than feeling the desire and capacity for greatness, but lacking a plan to unlock your latent potential. Devoting one hour every week to reflection is a small commitment compared to the insights you'll gain from these sessions. It's a smart investment in yourself that will improve your ability to deliver results and ultimately get more of what you want. Commit *today* to a new and better you—and then work hard to make it happen.

CONCLUSION

A Few Words of Wisdom

Thank you for reading *The 40 Best Sales Techniques Ever*. I hope that you found it to be very interesting and extremely helpful. And, of course, that you've begun to apply *The 40 Best* in your daily sales routine. Keep working at it, because these techniques *will* make you a sales superstar.

As a new author with a small publishing house, I rely on you—my readers—to spread the word. If you enjoyed this book, please tell your colleagues and friends. If you're a sales manager, buy copies for your team. Finally, if it's not too much trouble, I'd appreciate a glowing review on Amazon!

Like most salespeople, I love to tell a good story. I believe we're defined by the choices we make; we can choose to be happy, ethical, balanced, and optimistic. I'll leave you with a story that made a strong impression on me.

We're all swimmers in my family, and we recently attended a banquet honoring the top junior swimmers in New England. The guest speaker was Olympian Elizabeth Beisel, who told the story of her swimming odyssey. Elizabeth made the U.S. National Swim Team at age 13, and at 15 she became the youngest member of the U.S. Olympic Swim Team at the 2008 Beijing Olympics. Now, at 24, she's already participated in three Olympic games. Over her swimming career, she's won eight medals: four Gold, one Silver, and three Bronze.

Elizabeth's coach always gave her challenges to keep her motivated: "You're going to qualify for the national team," "You're going to break the world record," or "You're going to win the Gold today." But what the audience didn't know was that these challenges served another purpose—to calm her nerves, which were ragged before big races. So much so, she told us, that before almost every race, she'd flee to the bathroom and throw up.

It was 2011 at the World Aquatics Championship, and as usual Elizabeth's stomach was doing double-backflips. She was seriously on edge. Sensing this, her coach approached her and issued another challenge, but this time it was different. "Have fun," he told her. "No matter what happens today, have fun."

As she reflected on her coach's challenge, Elizabeth felt liberated. During warm-ups, she was relaxed and loose, chatting with her fellow competitors. At one point, she took a moment to gaze out on the vast audience and really drink-in the moment. "*It's amazing that I'm even here*," she thought, "*and that I have this opportunity for greatness while doing something I love.*"

With Zen-like calmness, Elizabeth went on to win her race, posting the top qualifying time and beating her closest competitor by more than two seconds—a huge margin in competitive swimming. Those two simple words—*Have fun*—made all the difference in the world. With the pressure off, she performed at an even higher level.

I opened this book with a quote from Steve Jobs: *The journey is the reward.* I really believe this; even as I face new challenges and reach new plateaus in my career, I find myself looking back and thinking about how much I've enjoyed the climb. As Elizabeth Beisel demonstrated, simply reminding yourself to have fun and recognize how lucky you are can bring about a peace of mind that enables you to achieve *even greater things*.

I'm positive that your commitment to **The 40 Best** will transform both the way you sell and your ability to drive your own success. Great rewards await you. Oh, and before I forget—send me a note from the President's Club trip and tell me your story.

Good luck, good selling, and *have fun*!

Jonathan

WORK WITH ME

By reading this book, I hope you've gained knowledge to better prepare you for a **stellar** career in sales. There are a number of ways that you can do even more with *The 40 Best* to maximize their impact on you and your salesforce.

Training and Materials

I offer training on all of *The 40 Best* sales techniques. With a deeper understanding of how these winning techniques really work, salespeople are more focused, productive, and empowered to drive better results. I can also help your company create its own custom version of all the documents covered in this book: the Customer Starter Kit, Close Plan, Pilot Questionnaire, Pilot Charter, and more.

Sales Playbook

I can combine *The 40 Best* with your own internal best practices to create **a customized Sales Playbook** for your organization. This playbook will detail all of the best practices, approaches, and sales techniques that you want your salesforce to deploy to win more business and increase revenue. Benefits include:

- Making new salespeople more productive faster.
- Driving even higher levels of performance among existing sales reps.
- Reducing ramp-up time for new hires.
- Aligning the entire salesforce around your way of selling (i.e., "the HP way").

Speaking Engagements

I'm an active speaker and would welcome the opportunity to speak at your sales meeting or event.

For more information:

Email me at jonathan@the40best.com or fill out the Contact form on my website at www.the40best.com to learn more.

Jonathan Jewett

jonathan@the40best.com
Twitter: @salesinnovate
Facebook: jonathanjewettfan
www.the40best.com

ACKNOWLEDGEMENTS

I'd first like to thank my family: Marianne, Cambria, and Dylan (*"You're working on your book again? Am I going to be in it?"*). I love you all, and appreciate your patience with me as I completed this project. To my Mom, Todd, Chris, Greg and the other members of my extended family, thank you for all your input and support.

Thanks also to Brad Kayton, Bill Hershberger, and Lance Knight for your quotes, feedback and willingness to review and comment on the various revisions I sent you. You helped me to make this a better book.

Thank you to my editor Patricia Bull, who has been terrific to work with. I would highly recommend Patricia to my fellow authors. Patricia lives in Cambridge MA (Harvard and MIT territory!), and may be reached through email at pb47design@yahoo.com.

Thanks also to Helen Chang at Author Bridge Media (www.authorbridgemedia.com) for her branding wisdom and support. I very much enjoyed working with Helen and can't recommend her highly enough.